An action guide for
conscious consumers

Take It Personally
...

1 – ACTIVISM

With democracy in decline, activism has become the new means of political expression in the 21st century. From the watershed that was Seattle to the way both sides use the Web, the value of civil disobedience Ruckus-style to the response of governments and the likes of the WTO, we look at the issues that are shaping the global anti-corporate network.

2 – PEOPLE

A new world order that places money above all else is ignoring one vital point – people matter. Workers in the developing countries are not simply numbers to be used as sweatshop fodder; children are not brought into this world to serve as free labor, sex slaves, or soldiers. The end result of ignoring the needs of individuals, communities, and countries is misery and poverty for millions across the globe.

3 – DEVELOPMENT

Progress, development, an end to poverty – all have been cited as pots of gold at the end of the globalization rainbow. Yet time and time again the needs, aspirations, and varying cultures of the developing world are blatantly ignored in the drive to push the true agenda – opening up new opportunities for the developed world to exploit its poorer relations in the South.

4 – ENVIRONMENT

No issue is more pressing than the havoc we are wreaking on our planet. From cutting down the rainforests to selling off our water supplies to the highest bidder, polluting our atmosphere with exhaust fumes and contaminating our food with GMOs, we are planting a time-bomb that will explode with catastrophic results. Be warned – we are already seeing the first signs.

5 – MONEY

Money, it seems, is everything. The huge relentless wheel that is global capitalism is driven by faceless, unaccountable bureaucrats and businessmen who seem deaf to the needs of individuals, communities, indeed whole nations. Yet it takes little imagination to see that this situation is unsustainable if we wish to have a planet that is worth living in, and not one where the developed world becomes a fortress to repel the needs of poorer nations.

Civil **disobedience** is **not** our problem.
Our **problem** is civil **obedience**.

Our problem is that numbers of people all over the world have obeyed the dictates of the leaders of their government and have gone to war, and millions have been killed because of this obedience...

Our problem is that people are obedient all over the world in the face of poverty and starvation and stupidity and war and cruelty.

Our problem is that people are obedient while the jails are full of petty thieves, and all the while the grand thieves are running the country.

That's our problem.

> **Howard Zinn**

TAKE IT PERSONALLY

Anita Roddick

I have devoted most of my working life to finding new ways of doing business, and the last ten years at least looking for ways for business to take a lead in making the world a better place. If the world of commerce and finance seem impersonal sometimes, this has been my way of taking it personally. It wasn't that I wanted business-people to take over the role from governments and communities, just that – more than any other generation and any other sector – it seemed to me that business was in a powerful position to make a difference.

I still believe what we did at The Body Shop was worthwhile, and I'm proud of my involvement in it and the successes we had – however small they've been compared to the scale of the problem. But over the last year or so, I have come to realize that the great leap forward in understanding around the world just hasn't happened. I realized that, far from moving in a better direction for the planet, taking up their responsibility for our social and environmental health, business has become trapped in an international regime – almost a belief system – which has seriously constricted all our ambitions. That system has become known as globalization.

At its heart is a secretive system of impersonal, international committees and cabals, but for the vast majority of the world it's a very personal business – affecting their livelihoods, families, and environments. It's become personal for me too. This book is the result of that past year of rising awareness by me, and by others all over the world. It's a bold attempt to popularize the issues, to put them in context and find out how we got into this situation – and what we can do about it.

Like every modern phenomenon you can think of, globalization is a massive jumble of contradictory trends, of the hopeful and the hopeless, the humane and the barbarous. It is like the opening of A Tale of Two Cities, the best of times and the worst of times.

It is the most important change in the history of mankind, and often just the latest name for the conspiracy of the rich against the poor. It is the phenomenon most subject to the efforts of econometricians and statisticians, and the least understood and measured change in our time.

This last paradox is particularly important, because – although we know vast amounts about the flow of capital and spending power around the world, and the figures fill the media every day – we also see very little reflection of the personal experience of globalization by ordinary people around the world. We see the Wall Street traders; we don't see the sweatshop workers or the farmers driven from their land. We see the joy but not the misery.

This is an important omission, because it is people's personal experience of the phenomenon that really counts. Not just for the poor, but for all of us. In the end, we all have to take globalization personally.

I think I can say in all modesty that I've been to some places in the world that most CEOs would never dream of going. Often in search of new products, sometimes just for the hell of it, sometimes just to see for myself what's really going on. I'm probably one of the few international retailers to be baton charged and tear-gassed by American policemen during the WTO meeting in Seattle in November 1999.

As a result of this experience, I've held mutated babies genetically handicapped by toxic waste dumped in local streams. I've spied on illegal loggers in Sarawak. I've seen babies living near Mexican tobacco fields that were born without genitalia – and if anything made me take it personally, that did. The Mexican example was particularly shocking – and not just for me. Scientists had tracked down the cause to the pesticides, but the American tobacco companies that bought the crops grown there wouldn't accept responsibility, because they said the fields didn't belong to them. And knowing that representatives of these companies would be in a Cancun conference I spoke at about it, I showed them the slides.

This kind of confrontation isn't always the best way of going about creating change. But there was absolutely no reaction from them at all: no embarrassment, no outrage, just a bloodless sense of good manners.

I'm occasionally accused of seeing these issues too personally. As if being in business was necessarily a cold-hearted, objective, pseudo-scientific project to manipulate consumers. But I've also learned over the years that it can't be that any more. The future of the world depends on us all taking it personally. I was chilled by the experience in Cancun partly because they didn't, and partly because these were no ordinary people. As world business leaders, they were probably some of the few individuals in the world who could do something about it.

Unfortunately, the leaders of globalization – as set out in this book – have tied themselves to a single measurement by which they judge success and failure, and which is too narrow to recognize personal testimony. They only measure money and the bottom line.

This perverse idea, that only money counts in business, has reached its apotheosis in the World Trade Organization – recognizing profit and loss, but not human rights, child labor, or the environment. If the WTO is our new, unelected world government, then it is government without a heart, and without a heart you find the creativity of the human spirit dwindles too. The result is devastated forests, chemically-mutated babies, child slaves, and a situation where – even in Thailand – there are more prostitutes than monks.

Only measuring money is a kind of survival of the economically fittest. But their interpretation of the "fit" – the marketable, the profitable, the global – is pathetically inadequate. It's a kind of fascism, really – I don't think that's putting it too strongly – just as fascism was a perversion of Darwin's survival theories. The financially "fit" survive. Those that don't fit – people, communities, and nations – are bled dry. It's a devastating machine that can bear no variation, and it isn't building the kind of world most of us want.

The corporate pioneer John D. Rockefeller once boasted that he was quite willing to pay someone a salary of a million dollars if they were brutal enough. "He must be able to glide over every moral restraint with almost childlike disregard," he wrote, "and has, besides other positive qualities, no scruples whatsoever and be ready to kill thousands of victims – without a murmur." If you pretend that business is beyond morality, that's the kind of morality you get.

If civilization is going to survive, business and policy-makers must move on, to find within themselves more developed emotions than fear or greed. I believe we can only do that by letting ordinary people take more responsibility for running the world, and that means opening up these powerful and unbending institutions to a whiff of democracy. It means pulling down the globalization equivalent of the Berlin Wall.

That means, in turn, building a whole new set of democratic institutions, but it also means building up from below. I believe that we can see, in the rapid development of non-governmental organizations (NGOs), the start of that process happening already, as they start to give a voice to those excluded from globalization.

One question from Greenpeace by fax to a food manufacturer in 1999 was enough for them to take GM ingredients out of baby food. It was Indonesian NGOs that helped bring down the dictator President Suharto. There are now about 26,000 international NGOs – four times as many as there were a decade ago. But what was once a small band of charities raising money to help the occasional person rise a little out of poverty has grown into the vastly influential sector of the world.

What's more, by linking up with NGOs, there are companies out there who have already decided to go beyond their narrow – and sometimes non-existent – responsibilities under the law. We have the Co-op Bank refusing to invest in unethical business. We have Iceland breaking ranks to be the first major supermarket chain to ban GM ingredients, and promising to remove all artificial coloring from its own brand products. We have The Body Shop putting resources into building "community trade" – like its highly successful joint ventures with communities in India, Nepal, and Ghana. We now have 22 suppliers in 13 different countries, and many of those are informal groups of fair trade organizations. Often they use NGOs as suppliers.

Alliances between companies and NGOs are a powerful twist to what had originally been implacable opposition on both sides – but it isn't enough. Why? Because the most powerful bodies in the world, the World Trade Organization, the World Bank, and the International Monetary Fund, are also the least democratic and inclusive. The result has been a major democratic deficit that threatens the delicate consent that globalization has been able to operate under, and also – as it happens – threatens what progress the NGOs have been able to make. It means that half the people and about two thirds of the countries of the world lack full control over their own economic policy.

That situation isn't sustainable. As always in closed societies, it means the institutions are unable to change, to deal with mistakes, or to learn. The result is dangerous for all of us. World leaders from Nelson Mandela to Vaclav Havel welcomed the report of the Independent Commission on Global Governance in 1995, which proposed – among other things – an UN Economic Security Council, a Global Competition Office to deal with the rising power of multinational corporations, and a more democratic IMF. Five years on, the report has been buried away. The same fate has befallen all the other UN proposals to bring world finance under more democratic control.

But without more openness and democracy, the world will be unable to deal with the serious crisis brought on us by globalization – malaria in New York's Central Park, flooding in Yorkshire, Asian flu in the markets – let alone the abject impoverishment that makes globalization so personal to so many people.

We know the problems. I hope this book will in some way contribute to the shared solutions that will be the first steps toward those new democratic, global institutions.

Dedicated to the **activists**, the **grassroots organizations**, the **thought leaders** and the **alternative media** who challenge the myth of the global economy and especially to **Tony Clarke** (Director of the Polaris Institute in Canada) from whom I first heard the challenge **"Take it personally."** Also to **Ralph Nader** whose sense of the possibility of citizenship has been an inspiration to all of us.

Anita Roddick

ACTIVISM

Activism is my rent for living on this planet
Alice Walker

MYTH:

Democracy and Capitalism go hand in hand.

REALITY:

Democracy and market economies are exactly what we should be seeking, because they are the foundation of equitable, self-organizing societies. Capitalism is the mortal enemy of both. And it creates an illusion in the minds of the powerful that it is an engine of prosperity rather than an engine of destruction and upward redistribution.

By definition, design, and practice, capitalism is a system that concentrates economic power in the hands of the few to the exclusion of the many.

Anita: If there was one moment when the real disaster of globalization came home to me, it was in Seattle — in the violence and confusion on the streets outside the failed Ministerial Meeting of the World Trade Organization. Day after day, no matter what the police threw at them, they kept on coming back — more determined, more passionate, and more resourceful every time. It was an extraordinary experience, a frightening glimpse of what corporate-controlled reality might look like with its black-clad police, and I'll never forget it. And at the height of the confusion, with teargas and pepper in my eyes, I ran into the author Paul Hawken, momentarily blinded. This is how he described what might emerge one day as a turning point in history...

When I was able to open my eyes, I saw lying next to me a young man, 19, maybe 20 at the oldest. He was in shock, twitching and shivering uncontrollably from being tear-gassed and pepper-sprayed at close range. His burned eyes were tightly closed, and he was panting irregularly. Then he passed out. He went from excruciating pain to unconsciousness on a sidewalk wet from the water that a medic had poured over him to flush his eyes.

Paul Hawken More than 700 organizations and between 40,000 and 60,000 people took part in the protests against the WTO's Third Ministerial on November 30 1999. That morning, I walked towards the Convention Center with Randy Hayes, the founder of Rainforest Action Network. As soon as we turned the corner on First Street and Pike Avenue, we could hear drums, chants, sirens, roars. At Fifth, police stopped us. We could go no further without credentials. Ahead of us were thousands of protesters. Beyond them was a large cordon of gas-masked and riot-shielded police, an armored personnel carrier, and fire trucks. On one corner was Niketown. On the other, the Sheraton Hotel, through which there was a passage to the Convention Center. The cordon of police in front of us tried to prevent more protestors from joining those who blocked the entrances to the Convention Center.

Randy was a credentialed WTO delegate, which means he could join the proceedings as an observer. He showed his pass to the officer who thought it looked like me. The officer joked with us, kidded Randy about having my credential and then winked and let us both through. Ahead of us crowds were milling and moving.

Opening ceremonies for the WTO's Third Ministerial were to have been held that Tuesday morning at the Paramount Theater near the Convention Center. Mayor Paul Schell stood despondently near the stage. Since no scheduled speakers were present, Kevin Danaher, Medea Benjamin, and Juliet Hill from Global Exchange went to the lectern and offered to begin a dialogue in the meantime. The WTO had not been able to come to a pre-meeting consensus on the draft agenda. The NGO community, however, had drafted a consensus agreement about globalization — and the three thought this would be a good time to present it, even if the hall had only a desultory number of delegates. Although the three were credentialed WTO delegates, the sound system was quickly turned off and the police arm-locked and handcuffed them. Medea's wrist was sprained. All were dragged off stage and arrested.

But while the Global Exchange was temporarily silenced, the main organizer of the downtown protests, the Direct Action Network, was executing a plan that was working brilliantly outside the Convention Center. The plan was simple: insert groups of trained non-violent activists into key points downtown, making it impossible for delegates to move. DAN had hoped that 1,500 people would show up. Close to 10,000 did. The 2,000 people who began the march to the Convention Center at 7am from Victor Steinbrueck Park and Seattle Central Community College were composed of affinity groups and clusters whose responsibility was to block key intersections and entrances.

There were no charismatic leaders barking orders. There was no command chain. There was no one in charge. Police said that they were not prepared for the level of violence, but as one protestor later commented, what they were unprepared for was a network of non-violent protestors totally committed to one task — shutting down the WTO. For WTO delegates accustomed to an ordered corporate or governmental world, it was a calamity.

Up Pike toward Seventh and to Randy's and my right, on Sixth, protestors faced armored cars, horses, and police in full riot gear. In between, demonstrators ringed the Sheraton to prevent an alternative entry to the Convention Center. At one point, police guarding the steps to the lobby pummelled and broke through a crowd of protestors to let eight delegates in. On Sixth Street, Sergeant Richard Goldstein asked demonstrators seated on the street in front of the police line "to co-operate" and move back 40 feet. No-one understood why, but that hardly mattered. No-one was going to move. He announced that "chemical irritants" would be used if they did not leave.

The police were anonymous. No facial expressions, no face. You could not see their eyes. They were masked Hollywood caricatures burdened with 60 to 70 pounds of weaponry. These were not the men and women of the 6th precinct. They were the Gang Squads and the SWAT teams of the Tactical Operations Divisions, closer in training to soldiers from the School of the Americas than local cops on the beat. Behind them and around were special forces from the FBI, the Secret Service, even the CIA.

The police were almost motionless. They were equipped with US military standard M40A1 double canister gas masks; uncalibrated, semi-automatic, high velocity Autocockers loaded with solid plastic shot; Monadnock disposable plastic cuffs, Nomex slash-resistant gloves, Commando boots, Centurion tactical leg guards, combat harnesses, DK5-H pivot-and-lock riot face shields, black Monadnock P24 polycarbonate riot batons with TrumBull stop side handles, No.2 continuous discharge CS (orto-chlorobenzylidene-malononitrile) chemical grenades, M651 CN (chloroacetophenone) pyrotechnic grenades, T16 Flameless OC Expulsion Grenades, DTCA rubber bullet grenades (Stingers), M-203 (40mm) grenade launchers, First Defense MK-46 Oleoresin Capsicum (OC) aerosol tanks with hose and wands, .60 caliber rubber ball impact munitions, lightweight tactical Kevlar composite ballistic helmets, combat butt packs, 30 cal. thirty-round mag pouches, and Kevlar body armor. None of the police had visible badges or forms of identification.

The demonstrators seated in front of the black-clad ranks were equipped with hooded jackets for protection against rain and chemicals. They carried toothpaste and baking powder for protection of their skin, and wet cotton cloths impregnated with vinegar to cover their mouths and noses after a tear-gas release. In their backpacks were bottled water and food for the day ahead.

Ten Koreans came around the corner carrying a 10-foot banner protesting against genetically modified foods. They were impeccable in white robes, sashes, and headbands. One was a priest. They played flutes and drums and marched straight toward the police and behind the seated demonstrators. Everyone cheered at the sight and chanted: "The whole world is watching." The sun broke through the gauzy clouds. It was a beautiful day. Over cellphones, we could hear the cheers coming from the labor rally at the football stadium. The air was still and quiet.

At 10am, the police fired the first seven canisters of tear gas into the crowd. The whitish clouds wafted slowly down the street. The seated protestors were overwhelmed, yet most did not budge. Police poured over them. Then came the truncheons, and the rubber bullets. I was with a couple of hundred people who had ringed the hotel, arms locked. We watched as long as we could until the tear gas slowly enveloped us. We were several hundred feet from Sgt Goldstein's 40-foot "co-operation zone." Police pushed and truncheoned their way through and behind us.

We had covered our faces with rags and cloth, snatching glimpses of the people being clubbed in the street before shutting our eyes. The gas was a fog through which people moved in slow, strange dances of shock and pain and resistance. Tear gas is a misnomer. Think about feeling asphyxiated and blinded. Breathing becomes labored. Vision is blurred. The mind is disoriented. The nose and throat burn. It's not a gas; it's a drug. Gas-masked police hit, pushed, and speared us with the butt ends of their batons. We all sat down, hunched over, and locked arms more tightly. By then, the tear gas was so strong our eyes couldn't open. One by one, our heads were jerked back from the rear, and pepper was sprayed directly into each eye. It was very professional. Like hair spray from a stylist. Sssst. Sssst.

As I tried to find my way down Sixth Street after the tear gas and pepper spray, I couldn't see. The person who found and guided me was Anita Roddick, the founder of The Body Shop, and probably the only CEO in the world who wanted to be on the streets of Seattle helping people that day. When your eyes fail, your ears take over. I could hear acutely. What I heard was anger, dismay, shock. For many people, including the police, this was their first direct action. Demonstrators who had taken non-violent training were astonished at the police brutality. The demonstrators were students, their professors, clergy, lawyers, and medical personnel. They held signs against Burma and violence. They dressed as butterflies.

The Seattle Police had made a decision not to arrest people on the first day of the protests – a decision that was reversed for the rest of the week. Throughout the day, the affinity groups created through Direct Action stayed together. Tear gas, rubber bullets, and pepper spray were used so frequently that by late afternoon, supplies ran low. What seemed like an afternoon lull or stand-off was because police had used up all their stores. Officers combed surrounding counties for tear gas, sprays, concussion grenades, and munitions. As police restocked, the word came down from the White House to secure downtown Seattle or the WTO meeting would be called off. By late afternoon, the Mayor and Chief announced a 7pm curfew, "no protest" zones, and declared the city under civil emergency. The police were fatigued and frustrated. Over the next seven hours and into the night, they turned downtown Seattle into Beirut.

That morning, it was the police commanders who were out of control, ordering the gassing and pepper spraying and shooting of people protesting non-violently. By evening, it was the individual police who were out of control. Anger erupted, protestors were kneed and kicked in the groin, and police used their thumbs to grind the eyes of pepper-spray victims. A few demonstrators danced on burning dumpsters that were ignited by pyrotechnic tear-gas grenades – the same ones used in Waco.

The police mandate to clear downtown was achieved by 9pm Tuesday night. But police, some who were fresh recruits from outlying towns, didn't want to stop there. They chased demonstrators into neighborhoods where the distinctions between protestors and citizens vanished. The police began attacking bystanders, witnesses, residents, and commuters. They had completely lost control. When President Clinton sped from Boeing airfield to the Westin at 1.30 am on Wednesday, his limousines entered a police-ringed city of broken glass, helicopters, and boarded windows. He was too late. The mandate for the WTO had vanished sometime that afternoon.

The next morning, and over the next days, a surprised press corps went to work and spun webs. They vented thinly veiled anger in columns, and pointed guilt-mongering fingers at brash, misguided white kids. They created myths, told fables. What a majority of media projected onto the marchers and activists, in an often-contradictory manner, was that the protesters are afraid of a world without walls; that they want the WTO to have even more rules; that anarchists led by John

Zerzan from Eugene ran rampant; that they blame the WTO for the world's problems; that they are opposed to global integration; that they are against trade; that they are ignorant and insensitive to the world's poor; that they want to tell other people how to live. The list is long and tendentious.

Patricia King, one of two Newsweek reporters in Seattle, called me from her hotel room at the Four Seasons and wanted to know if this was the '60s redux. No, I told her. The '60s were primarily an American event; the protests against the WTO are international. Who are the leaders, she wanted to know? There are no leaders in the traditional sense. But there are thought leaders, I said. Who are they, she asked? I began to name some, including their writings, area of focus, and organizational affiliations: Martin Khor and Vandana Shiva of the Third World Network in Asia, Walden Bello of Focus on the Global South, Maude Barlow of the Council of Canadians, Tony Clarke of Polaris Institute, Jerry Mander of the IFG, Susan George of the Transnational Institute, David Korten of the People-Centered Development Forum, John Cavanagh of the Institute for Policy Studies, Lori Wallach of Public Citizen, Mark Ritchie of the Institute For Agriculture and Trade Policy, Anuradha Mittal of Institute for Food & Development Policy, Helena Norberg-Hodge of the International Society for Ecology and Culture, Chakravarthi Raghavan of the Third World Network in Geneva, Debra Harry of the Indigenous Peoples Coalition Against Biopiracy, José Bové of the Confederation Paysanne Europèenne, Tetteh Hormoku of the Third World Network in Africa, Randy Hayes of Rainforest Action Network.

Stop, stop, she said. I can't use these names in my article. Why not? Because Americans have never heard of them. Instead, Newsweek editors put the picture of the Unabomber, Theodore Kaczynksi, in the article because he had, at one time, purchased some of John Zerzan's writings.

Paul Hawken is a businessman and author. He is also chairman of The Natural Step, an education foundation that advises on environmentally-sustainable business.

We don't fear **regulation**,
what we **fear** is customer **revolt**

 A Shell official

Anita: Naomi Klein's book *No Logo* has defined for the latest generation what the next battle is going to be about. It's about defining our lives in such a way that the giant corporations don't decide everything for us. Naomi and others like her are standing up for the human spirit, and our collective ability to say this to the big advertisers and mind-controllers: you will not think and feel on my behalf, you will not define my life on my behalf, you will not dominate the globe with your version of morality. But as Naomi says, that responsibility then falls back into our laps. We have to be able to say what kind of world we want. Protest just isn't enough – we need a vision...

Naomi Klein "This conference is not like other conferences." That's what all the speakers at "Re-Imagining Politics and Society" were told before we arrived at New York's Riverside Church. When we addressed the delegates, we were to try to solve a very specific problem: the lack of "unity of vision and strategy" guiding the movement against global corporatism. This was a very serious problem, we were advised. The young activists who went to Seattle to shut down the WTO and to Washington DC to protest against the World Bank and the IMF had been getting hammered in the press as tree-wearing, lamb-costumed, drumbeating bubble brains. Our mission, according to the conference organizers at the Foundation for Ethics and Meaning, was to whip that chaos on the streets into some kind of structured, media-friendly shape. This wasn't just another talk shop. We were going to give birth to "a unified movement for holistic social, economic, and political change."

As I slipped in and out of lecture rooms, soaking up vision galore from Arianna Huffington, Michael Lerner, David Korten, and Cornel West, I was struck by the futility of this well-meaning exercise. Even if we did manage to come up with a ten-point plan – brilliant in its clarity, elegant in its coherence, unified in its outlook – to whom, exactly, would we hand down these commandments? The anti-corporate protest movement that came to world attention on the streets of Seattle is not united by a political party or a national network with a head office, annual elections, and subordinate cells and locals. It is shaped by the ideas of individual organizers and intellectuals, but doesn't defer to any of them as leaders. In this amorphous context, the ideas and plans being hatched at the Riverside Church weren't irrelevant exactly, they just weren't important in the way they clearly hoped to be. Rather than changing the world, they were destined to be swept up and tossed around in the tidal wave of information – web diaries, NGO manifestos, academic papers, homemade videos, *cris de coeur* – that the global anti-corporate network produces and consumes each and every day.

This is the flip side of the persistent criticism that the kids on the street lack clear leadership – they lack clear followers too. To those searching for replicas of the sixties, this absence makes the anti-corporate movement appear infuriatingly impassive: evidently, these people are so disorganized they can't even get it together to respond to perfectly well-organized efforts to organize them. These are MTV-weaned activists, you can practically hear the old guard saying: "Scattered, nonlinear, no focus."

It's easy to be persuaded by these critiques. If there is one thing on which the Left and Right agree, it is the value of a clear, well-structured ideological argument. But maybe it's not quite so simple. Maybe the protests in Seattle and Washington look unfocused because they were not demonstrations of one movement at all but rather convergences of many smaller ones, each with its sights trained on a specific target. These smaller, targeted movements are clearly part of a common cause: they share a belief that the disparate problems with which they are wrestling all derive from global deregulation, an agenda that is concentrating power and wealth into fewer and fewer hands. Of course, there are disagreements, but, within most of these miniature movements, there is an emerging consensus that building community-based decision-making power is essential to countering the might of multinational corporations.

Despite this common ground, these campaigns have not coalesced into a single movement. Rather, they are intricately and tightly linked to one another, much as "hotlinks" connect their websites on the Internet. This analogy is more than coincidental and is in fact key to understanding the changing nature of political organizing. Although many have observed that the recent mass protests would have been impossible without the Internet, what has been overlooked is how the communication technology that facilitates these campaigns is shaping the movement in its own image. Thanks to the Net, mobilizations are able to unfold with sparse bureaucracy and minimal hierarchy; forced consensus and labored manifestos are fading into the background, replaced instead by a culture of constant, loosely structured and sometimes compulsive information-swapping. What emerged on the streets of Seattle and Washington was an activist model that mirrors the organic, decentralized, interlinked pathways of the Internet – the Internet come to life.

The Washington-based research center TeleGeography has taken it upon itself to map out the architecture of the Internet as if it were the solar system. TeleGeography says that the Internet is not one giant web but a network of "hubs and spokes." The hubs are the centers of activity, the spokes the links to other centers, which are autonomous but interconnected. It seems like a perfect description of the protests. These mass convergences were activist hubs, made up of hundreds, possibly thousands, of autonomous spokes. During the demonstrations, the spokes took the form of "affinity groups" of between five and twenty protesters, each of which elected a spokesperson to represent them at regular "spokescouncil" meetings. Although the affinity groups agreed to abide by a set of non-violence principles, they also functioned as discrete units, with the power to make their own strategic decisions. At some rallies, activists carry actual cloth webs to symbolize their movement. When it's time for a meeting, they lay the web on the ground, call out "all spokes on the web" and the structure becomes a street-level boardroom.

In the four years before the Seattle and Washington protests, similar hub events had converged outside WTO, G-7 and Asia Pacific Economic Cooperation summits. Each of these mass protests was organized according to principles of co-ordinated decentralization. Rather than present a coherent front, small units of activists surrounded their target from all directions. And rather than build elaborate national or international bureaucracies, temporary structures were thrown up instead: empty buildings were turned into "convergence centers," and independent media producers assembled impromptu activist news centers. When these events are over, they leave virtually no trace behind, save for an archived website.

The hubs and spokes model is more than a tactic used at protests; the protests are themselves made up of "coalitions of coalitions," to borrow a phrase from Kevin Danaher of Global Exchange. Each anti-corporate campaign is made up of many groups, mostly NGOs, labor unions, students, and anarchists. The groups remain autonomous, but their international co-ordination is deft and, to their targets, frequently devastating. The charge that the anti-corporate movement lacks "vision" falls apart when looked at in the context of these campaigns. It is true that the mass protests in Seattle and DC were a hodgepodge of slogans and causes. But in trying to find coherence in these large-scale shows of strength, the critics are confusing the outward demonstrations of the movement with the thing itself – missing the forest for the people dressed as trees. This movement is its spokes, and in the spokes there is no shortage of vision.

The student anti-sweatshop movement, for instance, has rapidly moved from simply criticizing companies and campus administrators to drafting alternate codes of conduct and building its own quasi-regulatory body, the Worker Rights Consortium. The movement against genetically engineered and modified foods has leapt from one policy victory to the next, first getting many GM foods removed from the shelves of British supermarkets, then getting labeling laws passed in Europe, then making enormous strides with the Montreal Protocol on Biosafety.

The fact that these campaigns are so decentralized is not a source of incoherence and fragmentation. Rather, it is a reasonable, even ingenious adaptation both to pre-existing fragmentation within progressive networks and to changes in the broader culture. It is a by-product of the explosion of NGOs, which, since the Rio Summit in 1992, have been gaining power and prominence.

There are so many NGOs involved in anticorporate campaigns that nothing but the hubs and spokes model could possibly accommodate all their different styles, tactics, and goals. Like the Internet itself, both the NGO and the affinity group networks are infinitely expandable systems. If somebody doesn't feel they quite fit in to one of the 30,000 or so NGOs out there, they can start their own and link up. Once involved, no one has to give up their individuality to the larger structure; as with all things online, we are free to dip in and out, take what we want and delete what we don't. It is a surfer's approach to activism reflecting the Internet's paradoxical culture of extreme narcissism coupled with an intense desire for external connection. One of the great strengths of this model of laissez-faire organizing is that it has proven extraordinarily difficult to control. It responds to corporate concentration with a maze of fragmentation, to globalization with its own kind of localization, to power consolidation with radical power dispersal.

Joshua Karliner of the Transnational Resource and Action Center calls this system "an unintentionally brilliant response to globalization." And because it was unintentional, we still lack even the vocabulary to describe it.

Of course, this system has its weaknesses too, and they were on full display on the streets of Washington during the anti-World Bank/IMF protests. At around noon on April 16 2000, the day of the largest protest, a spokescouncil meeting was convened for the affinity groups that were in the midst of blocking all the street intersections surrounding the headquarters of the World Bank and the IMF. The intersections had been blocked since 6am, but the delegates, the protesters had just learned, had slipped inside the police barricades before 5am. Given this new information, most of the spokespeople felt it was time to give up the intersections and join the official march at the Ellipse. The problem was that not everyone agreed: a handful of affinity groups wanted to see if they could block the delegates on their way out of their meetings. The compromise the council came up with was telling. "OK, everybody listen up," Kevin Danaher shouted into a megaphone. "Each intersection has autonomy. If the intersection wants to stay locked down, that's cool. If it wants to come to the Ellipse, that's cool too. It's up to you."

This was impeccably fair and democratic, but there was just one problem – it made absolutely no sense. Sealing off the access points had been a co-ordinated action. If some intersections now opened up and other intersections stayed occupied, delegates on their way out of the meeting could just hang a right instead of a left, and they would be home free. Which, of course, is precisely what happened.

As I watched clusters of protesters get up and wander off while others stayed seated, defiantly guarding... well, nothing, it struck me as an apt metaphor for the strengths and weaknesses of this nascent activist network. There is no question that the communication culture that reigns on the Net is better at speed and volume than at synthesis. It is capable of getting tens of thousands of people to meet on the same street corner, placards in hand, but is far less adept at helping those same people to agree on what they are really asking for before they get to the barricades – or after they leave. For this reason, an odd sort of anxiety has begun to set in after each demonstration: Was that it? When's the next one? Will it be as good, as big? To keep up the momentum, a culture of serial protesting is rapidly taking hold. My inbox is cluttered with entreaties to come to what promises to be "the next Seattle." Someone posted a message on the organizing e-mail list for the Washington demos: "Wherever they go, we shall be there!" But is this really what we want – a movement of meeting-stalkers, following the trade bureaucrats as if they were the Grateful Dead?

The prospect is dangerous for several reasons. Far too much expectation is being placed on these protests: Seattle's direct-action tactics worked because they took the police by surprise. That won't happen again. Police have now subscribed to all the e-mail lists.

In an attempt to build a stable political structure to advance the movement between protests, Danaher has begun to fundraise for a "permanent convergence center" in Washington. The International Forum on Globalization, meanwhile, is producing a set of principles and priorities, an early attempt, as Jerry Mander puts it, at "defining a new architecture" for the global economy. Like the conference organizers at the Riverside Church, however, these initiatives will face an uphill battle. Most activists agree that the time has come to sit down and start discussing a positive agenda – but at whose table, and who gets to decide?

These questions came to a head at the end of May 2000 when Czech President Vaclav Havel offered to "mediate" talks between World Bank president James Wolfensohn and the protesters planning to disrupt the Bank's September meeting in Prague. There was no consensus among protest organizers about participating in the negotiations at Prague Castle, and, more to the point, there was no process in place to make the decision: no mechanism to select acceptable members of an activist delegation (some suggested an Internet vote) and no agreed-upon set of goals by which to measure the benefits and pitfalls of taking part. If Havel had reached out to the groups specifically dealing with debt and structural adjustment, like Jubilee 2000 or 50 Years Is Enough, the proposal would have been dealt with in a straightforward manner. But because he approached the entire movement as if it were a single unit, he sent those organizing the demonstrations into weeks of internal strife. Part of the problem is structural. Among most anarchists, who are doing a great deal of the grassroots organizing (and who got online way before the more established Left), direct democracy, transparency, and community self-determination are not lofty political goals, they are fundamental tenets governing their own organizations. Yet many of the key NGOs, though they may share the anarchists' ideas about democracy in theory, are themselves organized as traditional hierarchies.

So how do you extract coherence from a movement filled with anarchists, whose greatest tactical strength so far has been its similarity to a swarm of mosquitoes? Maybe, as with the Internet itself, you don't do it by imposing a preset structure but rather by skillfully surfing the structures that are already in place. Perhaps what is needed is not a single political party but better links among the affinity groups; perhaps rather than moving toward more centralization, what is needed is further radical decentralization.

When critics say that the protesters lack vision, what they are really saying is that they lack an overarching revolutionary philosophy on which they all agree. That is absolutely true, and for this we should be extraordinarily thankful. It is to this young movement's credit that it has as yet fended off all of the competing agendas and has rejected everyone's generously donated manifesto, holding out for an acceptably democratic, representative process to take its resistance to the next stage. Perhaps its true challenge is not finding a vision but rather resisting the urge to settle on one too quickly. If it succeeds in warding off the teams of visionaries-in-waiting, there will be some short-term public relations problems. Serial protesting will burn some people out. Street intersections will declare autonomy. And yes, young activists will offer themselves up like lambs – dressed, frequently enough, in actual lamb costumes – to the *New York Times* Op-Ed page for ridicule.

But so what? Already, this decentralized, multi-headed swarm of a movement has succeeded in educating and radicalizing a generation of activists around the world. Before it signs on to anyone's ten-point plan, it deserves the chance to see if, out of its chaotic network of hubs and spokes, something new, something entirely its own, can emerge.

Naomi Klein is a journalist, and author of *No Logo*.

Anita: The term "globalization" has come to mean something very specific, but the idea of an inter-connected world — linked by appreciation of each other's cultures and the ability to see injustice in the formerly darkest corners of the world — has a great deal of resonance for people like me. It maybe that the IT revolution makes this possible, but — according to Jerry Mander — we still have to be very vigilant. Because we can wake up one morning and find that the technology of this virtual, inter-connected world wasn't the liberating force we thought, but binds us ever more tightly under the control of the money men. Well, we've been warned...

Jerry Mander The computer revolution is a weird issue, because both sides seem to agree about it. They all think it's great. The corporations and the activists, the engineers and the artists, the Al Gores and the Newt Gingriches, the conservatives and the liberals all out-do themselves to articulate utopian visions of a computer-based society. Does that make you uneasy? Shouldn't we have learned by now to be wary of any "revolution" led by corporations and vice-presidents?

Even my own friends tend to side with the computers-bring-you-power argument. "You miss the point," they tell me. "Computers can help us communicate with like-minded types; we can get better organized against those big corporations. We can reach people all over the planet, and use e-mail to mobilize."

Some of my friends quote Kevin Kelly, formerly of *Whole Earth* and now of *Wired*. He argues that the computer revolution created a new political structure on the planet. The symbol of today should no longer be the atom, he wrote, but the web. According to his view the political center has been wiped out and an entirely new web structure "elevates the power of the small player," while promoting a new kind of pure democracy where we can be equal players in the global information game. Also it brings on a new "incipient techno-spiritualism."

Kevin's right on the last point: techno-spiritualism, though I favor the older kind that doesn't require mediation by machines. As for the idea that the old political center has been wiped out by our PCs and e-mail and that web politics has brought us a computer-enhanced democracy, let me ask this: shouldn't we call it "virtual democracy?" I think so. Because somebody forgot to tell the transnationals in Tokyo, New York, Brussels, and Geneva that the real power was no longer in the center, and that it was now out of their control. Two hundred corporations now control 28 percent of global economic activity. The computer has had a crucial role to play in this, as have the global trade agreements that have deregulated all controls on international banking, investment, and capital movement. Corporations are now free to use the new global technologies to move their assets around the world, instantaneously, at the touch of a key, without the ability of nation-states to observe, control, or slow them down.

Some people understand this, notably among the Right. Dr Joe Cobb of the Heritage Foundation once told me that because of technology, corporate-led globalization is "inevitable." It can't be stopped (presumably because technology itself "can't be stopped," yet another paradigm worth examining).

So what kind of revolution do we have here? To use terms like "empowerment" to summarize the effects of computers is to badly misrepresent what power is about in a real political and economic context. Computers do help individuals feel powerful or content and certainly they are useful – nobody denies this. But this does nothing whatever to balance the ultimate drift of technology, to help gather staggering new power in the hands of giant corporations, banks, and global trade bureaucracies, all made possible by these same instruments.

In my view, computer technology will eventually be understood by all of us, as it already is by the Right – as the greatest centralizing technology ever invented. For while we sit happily at our PCs editing our copy, sending our e-mails, designing our little web pages, transnational corporations are using their global networks 24-hours a day, at a scale and at a speed that makes our level of empowerment seem pathetic by comparison.

The giant transnationals of today simply cannot exist without the global computer networks. When they push their computer keys they cause hundreds of billions of dollars to move from, say, a bank in Geneva to Sarawak, resulting in a forest cut down. Somewhere else they push a key and buy billions of dollars of national currency, only to sell it again a few hours later, leaving countries' economies in shambles, and populations devastated. That is information with power. Information by itself is for the disempowered and the Internet is our opiate.

The question we have to learn to ask about new technology is not whether it benefits us, but whom does it benefit most? For despite its usefulness to us in many activities, the electronic revolution has far more to offer the largest enterprizes on the planet than it does to you and me; we suffer a net loss from its emergence as the new global nervous system.

If you want to use your computers for your various good works, okay. But please keep in the forefront of your mind who else is using this wonderful "decentralizing" instrument, to what ends and with what results. And let's stop calling them empowering.

Jerry Mander is program director for the Foundation for Deep Ecology, president of the International Forum on Globalization (IFG), and senior fellow at Public Media Center — a non-profit advertising company highlighting environmental and social issues.

Technological progress has merely provided us with more efficient means for going backwards

 Aldous Huxley

Anita: Under the new Terrorism Act, you could be committing a crime by reading this page.

Zac Goldsmith

You know a political system is under serious threat when it resorts to draconian, authoritarian laws designed to shield it from even the mildest criticism. If that is true, then we in Britain should take heart from New Labour's Terrorism Bill, which came into force in February 2001. For contained within its statutes are laws so rigid that virtually every citizen of this country concerned about the path we are currently treading has at one point in their lives committed an act of terrorism.

The new Terrorism Act is an act of self-defence by a political system that understands the contempt in which it is held by its constituents. Recent events, like the protests against globalization or against the government's attitude towards the countryside, have pushed the government against a wall. In response it is building up its fortress, in the knowledge that with each concession made by our leaders to unelected corporations, the backlash will widen and more and more people not usually prone to such measures as civil disobedience will get involved.

The new Act effectively outlaws support for anything other than the status quo, and labels some of the greatest acts of defiance in history as "terrorism." For terrorism has become a club where Saddam may now hold hands with Lord Melchett. How to join? Try wearing a T-shirt in support of the Free Tibet campaign. That might make you a "terrorist" under section 13 forbidding the "wearing of a uniform or items of clothing supporting a 'proscribed' organization." Though not technically "proscribed," any form of direct action protest against the Chinese attempt to render Tibetans a minority in their own land neatly fits the bill. If that fails, you could organize a mass-fax protest directed at Number 10 calling for a fair referendum on the Euro. It's important to synchronize though, so that "serious disruption of an electronic system" is achieved. Do that and you're in the club, possibly earning 10 years in the process.

Baking cakes for the fuel blockades could pass as "support" for a terrorist group. They were hopelessly criminal, according to the new definition of "terrorism" which includes "a threat of action where the use or threat is designed to influence the government." Providing blankets for road protestors would similarly fit the bill, their campaigns designed, as they were, to "advance a political, religious, or ideological cause," and caused "serious damage to property."

Which brings me back to Lord Melchett, another known terrorist. Despite being acquitted following his arrest for uprooting genetically modified crops, he was in clear breach of great chunks of the Act. And because we applauded his action, and that of his colleagues in other anti-GM direct action groups, we would have been nearly as guilty as he. Why? Because merely supporting such an action is deemed "terrorist."

Government actions, like the frequent bombing of Iraq, do not fall within the jurisdiction of the Act. But what of otherwise legal organizations making use of government-released information? If we were to advise our readers, for instance, that a swift visit to www.environment.detr.gov.uk, (a government website), would reveal names and addresses of areas destined to host trials of herbicide-resistant crops, would that be illegal? It would certainly enable our more active readers to engage in terrorist wrongdoing. And what if we advised our readers local to those areas that the decent thing to do would be decontamination? Would that be a direct abuse of this law?

Yet perhaps the most extraordinary aspect of the new Act lies in the fact that Labour, by passing it, have effectively classed their own heritage as terrorism. Back in 1887 workers in Britain washed their hands of the Tories and Liberals, both of which were seen to have failed them in their effforts to achieve representation at government level. Mounting agitation led to a ban on riots and disorderly conduct which in turn led more than 100,000 workers to gather in Trafalgar Square in London where they were set upon by police. Three died, 160 were imprisoned, and the Labour Party was effectively born.

The government tells us that the new law will only be used as a defense against extremes. But who is to judge what constitutes extremism? Surely the Act depends entirely on the neutrality of the government of the day? If that is so then why should we believe that any government is truly "objective." The very basis of government after all, is subjective views on how things ought to be. More likely, the new Act will be deployed after the dust has settled, and the people become accustomed to living beneath its shadow. This was the tactic employed on news of Dolly the sheep's "birth." Human cloning, we were assured, will never be allowed. Just months later, the tune has changed dramatically. In the case of "terrorist" organizations like Greenpeace, the biotech saboteurs, and the perilous fuel protestors, it is unlikely the law will be used to its maximum for fear of public outcry. But other less prominent organizations may not be so lucky. For merely a suspicion of wrongdoing gives the powers of lengthy investigation directly to the police.

There is, though, safety in numbers. And the sheer breadth of the new Act ensures that those in breach of it are in big company.

Still feeling left out? Not a problem. Simply pop a copy of *The Ecologist* into your pocket and show it round to others. That way, you will be in breach of section 58 which forbids "the collection of information that may be useful for the purposes of terrorism."

Zac Goldsmith, activist and editor of *The Ecologist*.

Anita: What went wrong? Why have some of the best minds in the world developed this system, and negotiated it painstakingly too, when it has had such disastrous side-effects? One reason is that the rich countries still want to weight the rules in their favor. They are promoting competition, but not the ubiquitous level playing field. One of the globalization-watchers I've learned to respect most is Martin Khor. His articles and detailed critiques have done more than almost anything else to reveal this hypocrisy and to generate opposition to the World Trade Organization's agenda in developing countries...

Martin Khor After five years of the World Trade Organization (WTO), the developing countries – at least the governments – had expected some benefits. Their biggest disappointment is that the benefits did not occur. Many of the agreements also have a transition period of five years before implementation, so the worst aspects are yet to come. Even so, developing countries are beginning to feel the pinch. As they formulate new national laws to take into account the Uruguay Round Agreements, they are coming to realize that the agreements contain many imbalances that harm them.

Developing countries have had to reduce their import duties after a grace period. Governments will be more and more prohibited from giving domestic and export subsidies to farmers.

In many countries, NGOs and farmers have expressed great concern that if the import duties have to go down progressively, while at the same time Europe and the US continue to heavily subsidize their exports, then the farmers in developing countries will face great competition from imports and their livelihoods will be threatened. Studies in the Philippines already show how cheaper imports due to liberalization are causing grave problems for Filipino farmers. The situation will get worse in the next five to ten years.

To anticipate these problems and counter them before we have a social disaster on our hands, NGOs like ourselves have proposed that differential treatment should be given to developing countries on grounds of food security and the protection of the livelihood of a large portion of the population. This would mean that all food produced in developing countries for domestic consumption should be exempted from the provisions of the Agricultural Agreement in relation to import liberalization and domestic subsidies.

There are other major repairs we would like to see at the WTO. One is the Trade Related Aspects of Intellectual Property Rights (TRIPs) agreement. The WTO is meant to be an organization that looks into liberalization.

The TRIPS Agreement does the opposite – it is a protectionist device to prevent the transfer of technology from transnational corporations to domestic firms of developing countries. It prevents domestic firms in developing countries from being able to absorb new and modern technology. It perpetuates the technological superiority of the big companies so they can have control of the market and keep consumer retail prices far above what they would otherwise be if there were the competition.

If we can't eject TRIPS from the WTO, there are many things that can be changed. Consider, for example, Article 27(3)(b) dealing with patenting of life forms. It should be changed to prevent companies in any country from patenting biological resources or knowledge that have already been in use in other parts of the world for generations. It should also be changed to prevent any country from patenting any kind of life forms or natural processes, including micro-organism and micro-biological practices. This would pre-empt forms of intellectual property protection that would restrict the rights of their farmers to save their seeds. There has been a proposal put forward by African countries in the WTO to that effect.

Another change would be to the Trade Related Investment Measures agreement – TRIMS. To repair this, developing countries should be exempted from the prohibition on investment measures like minimum local content for the use of local raw materials.

Finally, to repair the WTO agreements, there is the principle of special and differential treatment for developing countries. But wherever it appears in the WTO agreements, rich countries are not obligated to grant special and differential treatment. They are only required in most cases to try their best, what is called a "best endeavor." The developing countries have put forward very clear proposals that special and differential treatment should not be on the basis of best endeavor, but should be legally binding. And this principle should be applied to many of the existing agreements in the area of TRIPS, TRIMS, agriculture, and so on.

The objective of putting competition policy in the WTO by the developed countries is to crack open the markets of the developing countries so their big companies can enter in free competition with domestic firms. When an investment agreement seemed to be imminent, developing countries said: "To protect our domestic firms, we would also like to look at competition policy. We must have a competition policy arrangement that would restrict the big companies from practicing restrictive business practices or abusing their monopolistic powers to overwhelm domestic firms."

But when competition policy was put forward by Europe and the United States in 1996 at a Singapore ministerial conference, they proposed a totally different view. For instance, they argued that government monopolies are anti-competitive. If you have local firms that are given advantages by government, or if local firms are able to enjoy some privileges, that would be considered anti-competitive, and unfair to the foreign company that wants to take over the market.

The United States is quite clear on this. Charlene Barshefsky, the US Trade Representative, said at the Singapore conference of 1996 that the US aim in competition policy is to gain greater market access in developing countries for American companies. The EU said the usefulness of putting the competition policy in the WTO is that then we can apply WTO principles to the competition policy. The principles it mentioned are national treatment and liberalization. In other words, the EU wants to be able to ensure that developing countries do not have policies that favor the local companies.

The developing countries mean something quite different when they talk about competition policy. They mean how to curb the big monopolies that are now getting bigger from taking over the local markets of the world. They also mean how to prevent the abuse of anti-competitive practices, such as the abuse of anti-dumping measures used particularly by the United States.

But a new paradigm is going to emerge in the coming years, which is that trade liberalization can be good if it is accompanied by certain other factors and conditions. For example, liberalizing your imports can be good if you have local firms that can make use of the cheaper imports to export to the world. But the firms must already exist and be able to take advantage of markets elsewhere. Markets elsewhere must be able to absorb the goods that you are able to produce. And the conditions in the country must already be good enough in terms of technology, infrastructure, education of the work force, and so on. In countries where such conditions do not fully exist, then liberalizing imports would destroy local industry or farms. Nor would the country have the firms that would be able to export and counterbalance the cheaper imports. If the governments continue to pursue the wrong policies, it is up to us as citizens to take the lead and show the insanity of the present system and point the way to another system that is more accountable and more balanced.

We cannot press a country to liberalize before it is ready, because it will lead to a potential collapse of that economy. This is something that the WTO has to realize. The developed countries may want to export more to the developing countries, but if they don't have jobs and income and are not able to export, you are exporting to a country that is not able to import. In the end, you just end up with a world recession, which is what we are now seeing.

In the mind of the free-traders, the ideal situation would be zero industrial tariffs all over the world. But this would actually mean the death of local industry in many developing countries. The whole issue is whether we are going to have any domestic economy left in the developing world – either industry, services, or agriculture. The situation is going to worsen in the next five to ten years. In the end, the WTO will have to come to its senses – not because of any ideology, but because of what is happening on the ground – that outright, all-out, big-bang liberalization is a disaster for the majority of countries in the world, and that this disaster will boomerang back on the developed countries in the form of lost markets, political instability around the world, and so on.

The issue is whether we realize it now and change the way the WTO works and change the way the developed countries treat the developing countries. If we do that, then we will prevent a catastrophe from happening around the world. The alternative is we don't change. The developed countries keep pressing the developing countries to open up in every area, and at the same time prevent technology from reaching them.

Then there will be a major catastrophe – socially, politically, and economically. In the end, we will have new global institutions arising out of the settling down of that catastrophe. Out of that anarchic disaster, something will have to happen, but in the meantime a lot of lives will be lost, a lot of nature will be destroyed.

Martin Khor is director of the Third World Network, an umbrella group of NGOs based in Penang in Malaysia.

Those who make **peaceful** revolutions impossible **will** make **violent** revolutions inevitable

> John F. Kennedy

Anita: Action isn't always enough. It usually needs to be shaped and led to achieve its desired impact. That's why the Ruckus Society is so essential. Since 1995, it's been a training ground for activists. Ruckus has shown dozens of human rights and environmental organizations how to make their protests dynamic, inspiring, educational, and newsworthy. This last asset is double-edged — the kinds of protests that Ruckus orchestrates have helped drag vital issues into the public eye but at the same time they've made the organization highly controversial. It pays to remember that at the Ruckus Society's Action Camps, activists are coached in *non-violent* tactics and strategies. The emphasis is on attaining campaign goals safely and effectively. There have been more than 20 of these camps throughout North America, yielding more than 2,500 "graduates" who are helping redefine civil disobedience in the 21st century.

Marianne Manilov & John Sellers

Marianne Manilov: For people who don't know the Ruckus Society, how would you describe your organization?

John Sellers: We are a community of activists from lots of different movements that really specialize in the use of non-violent direct action.

MM: What is it that you do?

JS: Our main program is action camp. In action camp we bring one to two hundred people together for a week around an issue, like globalization or human rights. We spend 14–16 hours a day skill-sharing and training. We work on everything: non-violence tactics, media skills, community organizing, and strategy. We also do physical training: we build a four-storey scaffolding to teach people urban climbing techniques. We teach political theater, street blockades, and also some technical tree climbing for activists who are interested in defending large wilderness areas.

MM: Seattle is an important part of organizing history now in the US. What was your best memory?

JS: It was incredible. We hung a giant banner out over Seattle that had two one-way street signs, pointing in opposite directions, one said "WTO" and the other said "Democracy." We knew that the whole thing would be about people power versus corporate power. We hung the banner from a giant construction frame high up over downtown Seattle. There was a lot of security surrounding the construction sight and getting up there was hard. Of course, there was some dicey stuff!

MM: The wind?

JS: Yes, and it was cold, and I was asked to come in at the last minute and it was a major climb and [laughs] I was really out of shape. But we pulled it off.

MM: You were recently arrested walking down the street at the Republican convention in Philadelphia and then your bail was set at $1 million which was unprecedented for someone with misdemeanor charges. What happened?

JS: You have to remember that I was not involved in the organizing around the Republican convention, I had just been on vacation with my family who live near there. I was just walking down the street and a lieutenant from the Philadelphia police came up and arrested me.

MM: You were in jail for eight days and I know you've been in jail a great deal over the years. How has being in jail informed you about the prison system here in the US?

JS: My attitude has changed significantly having spent time in a lot of different jails in the US. We have two million people incarcerated, more than any country on the planet, more than China. I meet all kinds of people when I'm in jail. In the Midwest, it's Native Americans, in Texas it's Chicanos, and everywhere it's Black people, it's poor people. Since the US declared this "war on drugs" we've had a three-fold increase in our prison population. But it's more than prison, the entire system is racially biased. It's rigged to criminalize people of color and poor people. When I'm in jail with young people of color, they can name the five cops in their neighborhood and which three have it out for them personally. That's a horrible reality to grow up in, where you are guilty for who you are, for the color of your skin, for your income level, for where you live.

MM: Tell me a little bit about what you see as interesting in the globalization movement, not just here, abroad too.

JS: [chuckles] I think the globalization movement is abroad mostly. This movement is a global one and that we have a lot to learn until we are able to say that we are on par here in the US with folks who are working on this in the global South or in Europe.

MM: Where do you think this movement started? Do you remember those folks who climbed trees and blocked new roads being built in the UK?

JS: The Road Warriors, for sure. The place I really saw the corporate globalization movement have its watershed movement was the Zapatista uprising. I remember how poetic Marcos was. The timing and message they had was impeccable. The way they used the Internet from deep within the rainforest and brought the eyes of the world to this remote area in Mexico and challenged this misnomer called "free trade."

MM: Who else do you look at now?

JS: I look at the Indian farmers who have been turning back genetic engineering. I think the entire planet owns them a great debt right now. I'm also really inspired by the biotech warriors in Europe. They got England going and all of a sudden people from all over the English social structure were going into the grocery stores or pulling up crops.

MM: For people who can't get themselves to a Ruckus camp, where do they start?

JS: There are amazing websites now around the world for information. Nobody needs Ruckus. Anybody can bring people together locally, have a dinner, have a meeting and bring people who are working on different issues and with different skills together and take on a local issue as a group.

www.ruckus.org

DEMOCRACY

WTO

RAINFOREST
ACTION NETWORK

Take it Personally

Political change requires a general sea-change in the attitudes of ordinary people

Spread the word

Political change requires a general sea-change in the attitudes of ordinary people. Talk to your friends and colleagues about globalization – point out that it is one of the most important issues facing all of us and communicate certain key messages, eg "we have lost our ethical footing," or "a healthy society involves a balance of power and globalization is putting too much power in too few hands" etc. And you don't have to have all the answers – just raise the questions. Ruckus runs a school of peaceful resistance and has lots of ideas on how to make your point using direct action without violence.

www.ruckus.org

Campaign

Support one of the many campaigns that seek to control globalization such as the World Development Movement, People and Planet, Friends of the Earth etc.

Change your lifestyle

Measure you and your family's ecological footprint and work to reduce it to the sustainable level. Focus on the action that makes the big differences (like cycling more instead of driving) instead of the small improvements (like recycling) – see People & Planet and Best Foot Forward websites.

Make ethical consumer choices

When you consume, make positive choices. Go organic. Buy Fair Trade. Eat less meat. Avoid multinationals. Support local businesses. Frequent your nearest farmers' market.

Be a pro-active employee

Raise responsible business practice with your employer – there are now a lot of good practice examples of progressive corporate behavior, eg socially-responsible sourcing, environmental auditing, ethical investment etc. (There is also a hard-core version of this message which says "don't work for corporate power" – ie at all.)

Lobby

Raise global justice issues with all decision-makers. Raise climate change with your local councillor or representative, international trade rules with your MP or Senator, Fortress Europe with your MEP, the US government's attitude to Kyoto with all political representatives etc etc. Help end the obsession with national issues. Check out www.progressivesecretary.org the Progressive Letter Writing Cooperative for a range of email campaigns you can join.

Invest ethically

Make sure ethically your money isn't working against justice. Bank and invest ethically. And check that ethical really means ethical (in your own terms).

Above all, connect to other people

It is very difficult to learn or act effectively on your own. Join other groups of people who are concerned about these issues (eg the campaign organizations above), and raise the issues in whatever contexts you operate in. If you are a teacher, include them in your classes on citizenship. If you are active in your local women's group or Women's Institute, talk about how globalization is hurting women in the developing world.

Mother Jones Online www.motherjones.com

Mother Jones is an independent, non-profit magazine that focuses on issues of social justice, the environment, politics, and popular culture. Renowned for its investigative reporting, the magazine has won eight National Magazine award nominations and three National Magazine Awards, has twice been named "Best in the Business" for investigative reporting by the American Journalism Review, and won the 2000 Alternative Press Award for General Excellence.

Adbusters www.adbusters.org

Adbusters magazine is the work of a global network of artists, activists, writers, pranksters, students, educators, and entrepreneurs who want to advance the new social activist movement of the information age. Their aim is to topple existing power structures and forge a major shift in the way we will live in the 21st century. Phenomenally impressive.

International Forum on Globalization www.ifg.org

IFG is a leading international voice directing public and media attention on the perils of economic globalization. Established in 1994, it is an international alliance of activists, scholars, economists, researchers, and writers from 20 countries formed specifically to stimulate new thinking, joint activity, and public education on global economic issues.

Mobilization for Global Justice www.A16.org

Good site for calendar events.

The Direct Action Network (DAN) www.directactionnetwork.org

DAN began as a coalition of activists groups working together to coordinate the N30 shut down of the WTO Seattle Ministerial. During the ten-day Convergence leading up to N30 a call was put out by an ad hoc "Post WTO" working group for N30 affinity groups to stay organized after N30 in the hopes of creating a continental network of activists.

Protest Net *www.protest.net*

This comprehensive protest site covers events by regions – including US, Canada, Europe, and Australia – as well as events by issues, covering all the usual suspects.

Progressive Letter Writing Cooperative *www.progressivesecretary.org*

Reclaim the Streets *www.reclaimthestreets.net*

This direct action group has gained widespread recognition over the last few years. From road blockades to street parties, from strikes on oil corporations to organizing alongside striking workers, its actions and ideas are attracting more and more people and international attention.

The Ruckus Society *www.ruckus.org*

Since 1995 Ruckus has been a training ground for activists. Ruckus has shown dozens of human rights and environmental organizations how to make their protests dynamic, inspiring, educational, and newsworthy.

Co-Op America *www.coopamerica.org*

Publishes *Boycott Action News*, listings of current corporate boycotts.

Computer Professionals for Social Responsibility *www.cpsr.org*

A public-interest alliance of computer scientists and others concerned about impact of computer technology on society.

Eat The Rich *www.e-t-r.net*

Truly anarchic site and definitely not one for the fainthearted. "Politicians are the scum of the earth. That's not an opinion. That's fact." A wide variety of stuff and an interesting take on the Universal Declaration Of Human Rights: "It's often cited as a stick to beat the uncivilized leaders of hostile governments, but never quoted in full. There are thirty articles in all, and if you look close enough you'll find that your government is pissing all over practically every single one of them..." Guaranteed to offend just about everyone.

2

PEOPLE

When spiders unite they can tie down a lion

Ethiopian proverb

MYTH:

Globalization will end poverty

REALITY:

Economic globalization creates wealth, but only for the elite who benefit from the surge of consolidations, mergers, global scale technology, and financial activity.

The rising tide of free trade and globalization is supposed to "lift all boats," and end poverty. But in the half century since this big push began, the world has more poverty than ever before, and the situation is getting worse.

Though the US is reaping the greatest benefits of globalization of any country, the benefits are not being shared. According to the IPS, American CEOs now earn 417 times the wages of factory workers they employ. Although unemployment in the US is low, the average worker is now earning 10 percent less, adjusting for inflation, than he or she did in the early 1970s. Globalization exacerbates this trend by setting workers against each other all over the world to keep wages low.

So much for the rising tide that lifts all boats. It lifts only yachts.

Anita: The terrible truth is that if nobody is watching and there are no enforceable international regulations about how we should do business — then even the cleanest and squeakiest corporations can transform themselves, almost unnoticed, into a force for evil. And if you peer into the sweatshops around the world, as I have — some of them well-lit, modern, and apparently civilized factories — you can see the by-products of an inhuman system. Charlie Kernaghan has seen more than most people. That's why he's one of the most potent voices against exploitation in the world...

Charles Kernaghan

How is it that so many giant companies, household names like Nike and Wal-Mart, have prospered so dramatically over the past decade whilst sweatshop workers from China to Nicaragua continue to be exploited?

Take, for example, the Indonesian workers who have been making Nikes for the past ten years. In 1991, they were paid US $0.45 per day, not enough to meet basic physical needs. Today, their inflation-adjusted wages are little better and mean that their living standards often remain as wretched as they were a decade ago. Nike, on the other hand, has tripled its annual revenues over the past ten years from $3 billion in 1991 to $9 billion last year. CEO Phil Knight got paid $3.2 million in cash last year, bringing his net worth to well over $5 billion and making him one of the richest men in the world. Despite the fact that Nike, giving in to pressure from human rights groups, issued a statement in 1998 promising to improve conditions for the 500,000 employees of their contractors, many claim that the situation has not significantly improved and the reality is but a shadowy reflection of that promise. Sweatshop workers are still being exploited and companies like Nike need to do far more to improve the situation.

Or take the Chinese workers who make Kathie Lee Gifford handbags sold by Wal-Mart, the world's largest retailer. A leading human rights watchdog discovered a factory in Zhongshan City in 2000 where workers for Wal-Mart's contractor are forced to put in 14-hour shifts, seven days a week, 30 days a month. They are effectively held as indentured servants in overcrowded dormitories. At the end of the month nearly half of them owe the company money – to cover two dismal meals a day and pay deductions for talking to co-workers while sewing. Over half of Wal-Mart's imports come from its contractors in China. Wal-Mart, like Nike, have argued that they do not permit their goods to be produced under sweatshop conditions and point to their requirement that suppliers sign a code of basic labor standards. They claim that when this has not been adhered to they have withdrawn production from that supplier. However, in February 2001 they were struck off the KLD Domini 400 "socially responsible" register, on the grounds that they had failed to ensure that their suppliers operate factories that meet adequate human rights and labor standards.

Why does this happen? Why does it continue? The answers: the culture of "profits before people" and in some cases government collusion. Many companies scour the globe to find the cheapest labor possible. They play countries off against each other in a bidding war for production contracts. In what has been dubbed "a race to the bottom," the winning contractors and governments are the ones willing to reduce their workforces to levels of pay and working conditions that strain human endurance to the limit. Some governments turn a blind eye to labor law violations, and the international human rights treaties they have ratified, and instead leave workers with little choice but to fall in line.

Take Indonesia, where human rights observers have noted the presence of army units inside some of the factories where Nike's shoes are made. Or Nicaragua, where workers were indicted by their government on charges that carry sentences of up to ten years in jail. Their crime: asking for an $0.08 increase per pair of blue jeans they assemble for retailers including Wal-Mart – jeans that sell in the US for $30 per pair.

Meanwhile, the accounting firms that companies (including Nike and Wal-Mart) use to monitor their factories – supposedly to ensure observance of international standards and corporate codes of conduct – often miss violations because their monitoring efforts are significantly flawed. Dr O'Rouke of MIT claims that auditing giant PriceWaterhouse Cooper, in its audit reports, failed to recognize workers' rights and, in some cases, overlooked serious violations of health and safety standards. Although PWC officials argue that their monitoring uncovered violations of minimum wage, overtime and safety laws, their shortcomings clearly indicate inadequate procedures.

When business journalists caught Wal-Mart lying in its denial of any connection to one particularly dreadful factory, the company's vice-president explained that it was because they were "defensive" about the sweatshop issue. Sweatshops are, indeed, indefensible. They insure that the great wealth created by the global expansion of trade and investment – touted by pundits the world over as the cure for poverty – remains with top corporate executives and shareholders while millions of workers barely survive.

Charles Kernaghan is the executive director of the National Labor Committee, an independent, non-profit organization focussed on the protection of worker rights.

Size 12

Made in Haiti
50% Cotton
50% Polyester
100% Sweatshop labour
4hour shifts, Seven day week
28 cents per hour
No right to speak out

Picture is of a model – used for illustrative purposes only

I work sixteen hours a day for a top shoe manufacturer

I get paid $50,000 per week

I work
sixteen hours
a day for a
top shoe
manufacturer

I get paid $15.00 per week

The Race to the Bottom

Anita: What's a day's work worth? Ask yourself that while you compare a corporate CEO's compensation with the daily wage of third world workers.

Charles Kernaghan

CEO vs Workers Compensation:

A sample of starvation wages around the world Hourly take home pay:		CEO 1998 Compensation (includes salaries, stock options, bonuses)	
Guatemala	37¢	Millard Drexler, GAP	$660 million
El Salvador	60¢		
Nicaragua	23¢	Phil Knight, Nike	$3 million
Honduras	43¢		
Haiti	30¢	David Glass, Wal-Mart	$40 million
Mexico	50¢		
China	28¢	Wal-Mart's Walton	
Indonesia	20¢	family is now worth	$67.5 billion
Burma	4¢		
Bangladesh	13-20¢	Nike's Phil Knight is worth	$5.8 million
Romania	17-37¢		
Russia	11-56¢		
US sweatshop	$3-$4		
US territory of Saipan	$3		

Can anyone live on these starvation wages?

The companies say, yes, for example, 60¢ an hour is a living wage in El Salvador, sufficient to raise a family. After all, El Salvador is not New York City.

We asked women workers who sew Nike garments in El Salvador if this was true. Could they survive on 60¢ an hour? "No, it's impossible," they told us. "It's a lie when the companies say that." Then they talked us through their daily expenses:

- **For an 8-hour day they earn $4.79**

- **It costs them 68¢ a day for a round trip bus fare**

- **A small breakfast – rice, beans, tortilla, and coffee is 80¢**

- **A modest lunch – rice, beans, and tortillas again, a scrap of chicken and lemonade, since they can't afford soda, comes to $1.49**

So, just getting back and forth to work and surviving costs them $2.97, leaving just $1.82 out of their daily pay of $4.79. The workers live in one-room hovels, 10 by 12 feet, sharing an outhouse and common sink with several other families. For this they pay $31.40 per month, $1.03 a day. That now leaves them with just 79¢ at the end of the day.

What do they do now? The cheapest supper for a family of three costs at least $1.14 – for rice, beans, tortillas, and coffee, and maybe the family splits a plantain. But they do not even have enough money for this. What about daycare, which costs $1.13 per day, or a child's new shoes which cost $8.00?

Women sewing expensive $75 Nike shirts are forced to raise their children on coffee and lemonade, since they cannot afford milk. No one can live on 60¢ an hour in El Salvador. It is a starvation wage. To climb out of misery and into poverty, the workers would need to earn at least $1.18 an hour. What would happen if Nike paid its workers $1.18 an hour rather than the current 60¢ wage? Would the sky fall in on corporate profits?

Hardly. At the 60¢-an-hour wage, the women are paid 20¢ to sew each $75 Nike shirt. At $1.18 an hour, the workers would be earning 39 1/2 cents for every $75 Nike shirt they sewed. This means their wages would still come to less than half of one percent of the retail price. Nike could surely afford that.

But it does not have to be that way

- **We can fight back**

- **We can remake our economy with a human face**

- **We can hold the corporations accountable to respect human and worker rights and to pay a living wage.**

This is not a boycott
It is the opposite. This is a struggle to keep jobs in the developing world, but jobs with dignity, justice, and fair wages.

We are winning!
Last year the companies said they would never agree to public disclosure, but that is exactly what university students have won on over a dozen campuses across the US including University of Michigan, Duke, and Georgetown. If a company wants to manufacture goods for these universities, it must now publicly disclose the names and addresses of its factories.

Today there is an active social movement of labor, religious, student, solidarity, and community organizations across the US, working together to end child labor and sweatshop abuses. Just five years ago, this movement did not exist. We have all come a long way.

Charles Kernaghan

Anita: Corporate crime kills far more people and costs taxpayers far more money than street crime.

David Korten For all the current focus on criminal justice in the United States, it is striking that no official statistics are compiled on corporate crime, though it is flourishing on a scale that makes most street crime seem petty by comparison. On a single day, June 15, 2000, *The New York Times* reported the following:

- Top executives of a life insurance company were accused in a lawsuit yesterday of enriching themselves by charging tens of millions of dollars in excess fees to the retirement plans that the insurer maintains for its workers and agents. Whilst the insurance company denies any wrong-doing, the lawsuit is still ongoing.

- Three former executives of CUC International [now Cendant Corporation] pleaded guilty to federal charges in what the authorities said was the largest and longest accounting fraud in history, continuing at least 12 years and costing investors $19 billion.

Include illness, physical injury, and death from dangerous, defective, and mislabeled products, dangerous working conditions, and the release of toxic pollutants, and the human and financial costs of organized corporate crime become truly staggering. Corporations also profit from facilitating crimes, as for example the money laundering facilities provided by major banking corporations to criminals and tax cheats, and the facilitation of cigarette smuggling by major tobacco companies. Yet, unlike the harsh mandatory sentences imposed on street criminals, often for petty crimes, the persons responsible for corporate crime rarely suffer personal fines or imprisonment.

Corporations profit not only from committing corporate crime and facilitating white-collar crime, they also profit from the punishment of street criminals. Prison operators have aggressively promoted the privatization of prisons globally.

David Korten is president of the People-centred Development Fund and board chair of The Positive Futures Network.

Corporate **crime** kills far more **people** and **costs** taxpayers far more **money** than street crime.

 Anita Roddick

Anita: As tourism shrinks the world, it opens up new opportunities for the sexual exploitation of the weak and vulnerable.

San Francisco Examiner "As many as 50,000 women and children are taken to the United States each year to be forced into prostitution, bonded sweatshop labor, and domestic servitude"

Nobee Saeieo thought she was going from Thailand to the United States as a $240-a-month cook, but she got much less than she bargained for. She was forced to cook meals, give manicures, and serve guests on her knees, 18 hours a day, seven days a week.

Dung, a 13-year-old from Vietnam, was sold to a silicon valley executive, who planned to use her to satisfy his sexual demands, federal prosecutors say. These are just two of the 150 people who federal prosecutors say have been victims of slavery or indentured servitude in the past five years.

Federal immigration officials say trade in slaves and indentured servants in the US is tragically common.

"It's thriving. It's very well-organized. It's very lucrative," said Mark Riordan, head of Northern California investigations for the federal Immigration and Naturalization Service. "It's a worldwide problem that shows up in every major city [in the US]."

"It's difficult for us to prosecute these cases," he said. "These are situations where the poorest and least sophisticated immigrants are being exploited."

As many as 50,000 women and children are taken to the United States each year to be forced into prostitution, bonded sweatshop labor, and domestic servitude, a State Department official estimated last year, citing a federal study that culled information from sources ranging from deportation statistics to organized crime trends.

In February 2000, a congressional committee heard testimony on a bill to increase punishment for people who smuggle or keep indentured workers in the United States.

"This modern day slave trade is appalling," said Rep. Chris Smith, R-New Jersey, a sponsor of the bill. "But even more appalling is the idea that we know about it, have the ability to slow and stop it, and we turn our heads."

Source: *San Francisco Examiner* Feb. 13, 2000

The test of **morality** of a **society** is what it **does** for its **children**

> Dietrich Bonhoeffer

Children's Rights

The United Nations Convention on the Rights of the Child (UNCRC) was drawn up in 1989 and gives children and people under 18 their own set of rights. Nearly every country in the world has signed up and agreed to the UNCRC. It has 54 Articles, including:

• You have the right to education and it should be free at primary level.

• If you're punished at school, your dignity must be respected. The aims of education are to develop your personality and talents, prepare you for life as a grown-up, and teach you to respect other people's rights. This includes learning to respect and tolerate different ways of life, different values, and the environment.

• You have the right not to do harmful work. Work should not stop you from learning, being healthy, or growing up. The government must set a minimum age when children can work, and make sure that you're not working in bad conditions.

• You have the right not to be sexually exploited or abused. No one has the right to do things to your body without your permission. Adults must protect you from prostitution and pornography.

• If you're under 15, you shouldn't have to fight wars or be in an army.

Articles 28, 29, 32, 34, 38 from Save the Children

Anita: Every day, 2,000 children around the world are killed or disabled by arms-related injuries. It's horrifying statistics such as this that galvanize the Campaign Against Arms Trade. Established in 1974 by a coalition of groups and individuals concerned about the growth in arms exports, it is committed to an end to the international arms trade and the UK's role in it as one of the world's leading arms exporters. CAAT is a campaigning and lobbying organization, but its research has also helped to expose the disproportionately high level of government subsidies for the UK's global arms companies. If "less private greed, more public good" has been one of the battle cries of the ethical business movement, CAAT's call for the re-orientation of the economy from military to civil production shouldn't be far behind.

Robin Oakley Imagine corporations with the power to decide between war and peace. Business doesn't get much bigger than that, which is why the globalization of the arms trade is of greater concern than other corporate sectors.

Whether we're talking about Shell or Nestlé, all types of multi-national corporations benefit by escaping national restrictions on their activities. With greater ability to move their operations and capital around the world, companies can pick and choose which laws they operate under and have greater influence with national governments than ever before. But when the product is weaponry, designed and built for the sole purpose of killing people, this becomes even more critical.

When weapons are sold, there is an endorsement implicit in the provision of one set of people with the equipment to kill another: we support your use of deadly force to achieve your aims. There is great motivation for the companies to perpetuate themselves and this situation. And if they've got the weapons, they've also got access to ministers and top level military information, which in turn

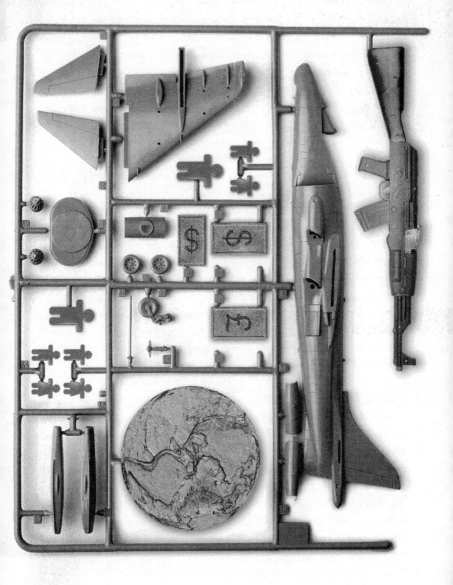

grants influence over national and global defense policy. And then, when arms companies begin to operate outside of national boundaries, they can play military powers off against one another. Hence their control over war and peace.

The power and influence of the biggest arms companies increase as they merge with or buy up competitors. By focussing their main business on the highest value elements of arms supply and outsourcing low-value, high-overhead processes like manufacture they are also hauling themselves higher up the value chain. For example, giants like BAe Systems (formerly British Aerospace) and Boeing now look so much further afield for their outsourcing, much to the dismay of smaller companies and unions in the US and UK, that Lockheed's F-16s have been described as the first "world fighter planes" because bits of them are made in a dozen countries, including Israel, South Korea, Turkey, and Taiwan (source: WPI, Arms Trade Research Centre Updates, Dec.99). One of the main objectives of industry consolidation is to make it easier for Western arms companies to sell weapons profitably around the world and to reduce competition, between companies and states, for the buying favor of soldiers and politicians in Asia, Africa, the Middle East, and Latin America. These sales beyond "the West" are seen as crucial to the industry; the bread and butter deals. They have the longer production runs, the lower development costs, and the inflated prices that are not present in NATO deals. It is in the regions of tension, conflict, regional arms races and highly militarized – usually human-rights abusing – states that there is greatest demand for weapons or the opportunity to create that demand.

While NATO/Europe is a significant market it has been financially dwarfed by sales to the Middle East in the last decade. It is no coincidence that the key destinations for UK weaponry are the Middle East and Far East where regional instability and tensions are keeping military spending high. Among recent targets for high pressure sales have been India and South Africa. In both countries the level of military spending is highly dubious when set against the levels of social provision and developmental achievement in education, health care, and nutrition. It's a high stakes industry. Single deals can make or break companies. At its height the notorious Al Yamamah deal with Saudi Arabia accounted for over 75% of all UK arms exports on its own.

This explains the enormous push to get big package deals made, often with massive government backing and incentives like off-set deals, commission payments, and licensed production. Licensed production is where equipment is partially or completely manufactured in the buyer country. This ranges from using a guaranteed amount of locally-sourced components to the entire production taking place in the buyer country with just the technical means and know-how supplied. This damages the value of the deal to the UK or US economy and takes jobs away from the UK/US shop floor, but it also allows vendors to benefit from cheap labor and low labor and industrial standards.

And by buying stakes in these local companies as part of deals, or in parallel with sales, or merging with them to produce hybrids, the multi-national players have evolved into enormously powerful and complex international networks.

Robin Oakley is fundraising development co-ordinator, Campaign Against Arms Trade

The guns and bombs, the rockets and the warships, all are symbols of human failure

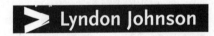 Lyndon Johnson

Global Exchange

www.globalexchange.org

Imagine if each time you went to visit relatives in another city or state you were subject to being searched and brutalized at military checkpoints. Imagine if by merely showing up to work you were threatened with jail or deportation. Imagine being unable to send your children to school because of policies enacted on Wall Street. Or imagine your employer forcing you to work 10–15 hours a day for only a few dollars. This is the stuff of nightmares, but daily reality for millions of people around the world.

Global Exchange, an international human rights organization working for global political, economic, environmental, and social justice, is responding daily to these kinds of abuses in the US and other countries. Through a versatile strategy to combat corporate globalization, Global Exchange is building people-to-people ties across borders and cultures to empower all peoples with the opportunity for peace and justice.

During the past decade many people around the world have been given new chances for democracy and justice as brutal governments, once propped up by the competing Cold War superpowers, have fallen. But daily repression and a climate of fear remain a reality for millions of people across the globe. Human rights abuses in war-torn Colombia are common, as an average of 12 political killings occur there every day. In the southern Mexico state of Chiapas the Mexican government has been brutally oppressive in response to communities' demands for the right to own the land upon which they live and work, and to govern themselves according to indigenous traditions and customs. And in Burma a military dictatorship continues to strangle the country's pro-democracy movement. Global Exchange has been involved in these and other countries, providing human rights observers to support local efforts for justice, peace, and democracy. By working closely with other human rights groups in these countries, international human rights observers play an important role in the peaceful resolution of conflicts.

But in a world where 51 of the largest economies are multinational corporations, many human rights abuses these days continue to be committed on the factory floor. Global Exchange is responding to this growing threat by exposing sweatshop abuses and demanding that corporations be held accountable for their actions. They target grassroots campaigns at corporations such as Nike and Gap, who despite some efforts to improve practices/wages for its suppliers' workers, have failed to rigorously enforce their promises. Global Exchange is pressuring corporations to put people before profits and increase the public's awareness of the need for greater corporate accountability.

Global Exchange strongly believes that economic security is just as central as basic rights protection to guaranteeing human dignity. But global rule-makers such as the WTO, World Bank, and IMF are promoting a "free trade" agenda that is undermining the economic security of hundreds of millions of people, advancing corporate interests at the expense of local communities, working families, human rights, and the environment. In response, a growing international movement has put elite decision-makers on notice that their destructive policies won't be tolerated any longer.

Global Exchange is working with other groups around the world to provide an alternative to the current system of economic inequality. The burgeoning Fair Trade movement is promoting a new model of global interaction, one based on cooperation, economic justice, and environmental sustainability, not exploitation. By purchasing Fair Trade products such as textiles, pottery, and coffee, consumers are assured that workers who export commodities to the US are being paid a living wage for their products. Fair Trade means community development, health care, education, and hope for the future.

What ties all this work together is the idea of "education-for-action," the belief that people must first have an immediate, personal understanding of injustice if they are to work to end it. Global Exchange's Speakers Bureau brings human rights and social justice activists from around the world to the US to educate audiences about political and economic oppression. Through Global Exchange's Reality Tours, individuals have the opportunity to journey to other countries to examine human rights situations firsthand. Similar study seminars in the US allow participants the opportunity to explore domestic human rights issues.

By taking a pro-active role in international issues that affect communities everywhere, Global Exchange is proving that governmental institutions and private corporations will not have the final say when it comes to political and social justice. We are providing the education needed to bring home the brutal realities of oppression and poverty. Thanks to our members' financial support and activist energy, we are building a new kind of grassroots internationalism that transcends borders and links people together with a common vision of a more just, sustainable world.

building people-to-people ties

Victoria's Secret

JC Penny, Victoria's Secret, IBM, Toys R Us, and TWA are among the US corporations that have profited by employing prisoners. Put together long mandatory sentences for minor drug offences, a strong racial bias, **prisons run by corporations for profit,** the sale of convict labor to corporations, and a charge for prison room and board and you have a modern system of **bonded labor – a social condition otherwise known as slavery.**

Take it Personally

If you have no confidence that the company is treating its workers fairly, don't buy from them

Every time you buy something consider it a vote of confidence in the company that produced it. So if you have no confidence that the company is treating its workers fairly, don't buy from them. Or if you must, send them a letter or e-mail. Big companies hate getting complaints from their customers, and if you can get your friends to join in – all the better.

A lot of companies say they are fair to their workers, but in fact turn a blind eye to bad working conditions, child labor, and starvation wages. Don't believe the PR. Check how companies are really behaving. As usual the web is a great place to do this quickly. Try the organizations that deal specifically with sweatshop issues such as The National Labor Committee, the Worker Rights Consortium, and Sweatshop Watch.

United Students Against Sweatshops

July 10-12, 1998: Students from twenty campuses across the United States met in New York City and formed United Students Against Sweatshops (USAS). The national coalition of student-based anti-sweatshop groups has energized the social justice movement with their ability to organize, negotiate, and take direct action (such as sit-ins) which have forced schools to adopt codes of conduct requiring full public disclosure. Now USAS is represented at over 100 schools and is crossing borders; in February 1999 a similar organization was formed by students in Canada.

Reebok releases independent report

Widely touted as a major turning point for corporations, last fall Reebok released a third-party report on two factories in Indonesia that employ almost 10,000 people. Reebok does not own the factories, but together they represent 70 percent of its total footwear production.

The company hired a Jakarta-based independent research and consulting firm to inspect the plants, observe working procedures, and interview workers. The assessment was based on standards set by Indonesian law and Reebok's human rights production standards. After a 14-month review, the independent researcher and Reebok released the Peduli Hak ("Caring for Rights" in Indonesian) report, which criticizes how factory managers communicate with workers; found that it was more difficult for women than men to obtain promotions; and found that health and safety procedures were less than exemplary.

In an op-ed piece for the *Washington Post*, Reebok CEO Paul Fireman wrote: "We think it's time to confront and accept responsibility for correcting the sometimes-abusive conditions in factories overseas. We'd like to encourage other multinational companies to follow suit." Mattel released a report from its Mattel Independent Monitoring Council (MIMCO) a month after Reebok. For a copy of Reebok's report, write to Reebok Human Rights Programs, 100 Technology Center Drive, Stoughton, MA 02072 or go to www.reebok.com

Big business "losing fight to militants"

Activists "represent a growing threat to organizations of all shapes and sizes," says a recent report. By "generating bad publicity and encouraging boycotts, they cause severe disruption, including damage to reputation, sales, profitability, employee satisfaction and share price." Big companies "tend to be unprepared, do not know how to respond and either fail to respond at all or respond ineffectively to activist groups. They have a tendency to bury their heads in the sand and hope the activists will go away. All the evidence is they don't."

There are 30,000 direct action groups targeting small private firms, as well as global giants. By ignoring activists or dismissing their arguments as unworthy of response, firms "effectively hand control over to them, allowing issues to spiral out of control." "Groups prosper when threatened. In a David versus Goliath battle, the public often sides with David. An organization's reputation can be badly damaged by being publicly presented as a bully." Companies including BP, Shell, Monsanto, and McDonald's have lost hundreds of millions of pounds after successful campaigns by direct activists against their business practices.

John Arlidge *The Observer*, Jan 21 2002

The National Labor Committee *www.nlc.org*

The National Labor Committee's mission is to educate and actively engage the US public on human and labor rights abuses by corporations. Through this education and activism, its goal is to end labor and human rights violations, ensure a living wage tied to "a basket of needs," and help workers and their families live and work with dignity.

Amnesty International *www.amnesty.org*

Amnesty International is a worldwide campaigning movement that works to promote all the human rights. Amnesty International campaigns to free all prisoners of conscience; ensure fair and prompt trials for political prisoners; abolish the death penalty, torture, and other cruel treatment of prisoners; end political killings and "disappearances;" and oppose human rights abuses by opposition groups.

Amnesty International has around a million members and supporters in 162 countries and territories. Activities range from public demonstrations to letter-writing, from human rights education to fundraising concerts, from individual appeals on a particular case to global campaigns on a particular issue.

The Worker Rights Consortium *www.workersrights.org*

This is a non-profit organization that supports and verifies licensee compliance with production codes of conduct. These codes of conduct have been developed by colleges and universities across the US to ensure that goods are produced under conditions that respect the basic rights of workers. WRC is developing a network of local organizations in regions where licensed goods are produced which will allow the WRC to inform workers of their rights and allow workers to report conditions securely and confidentially.

Sweatshop Watch *www.sweatshopwatch.org*

This is a coalition of labor, community, civil rights, immigrant rights, women's, religious, and student organizations, and individuals, committed to eliminating sweatshop conditions in the global garment industry. It believes that workers should be earning a living wage in a safe and decent working environment, and that those who benefit the most from the exploitation of sweatshop workers must be held accountable. Great links page.

Free Tibet   *www.freetibet.org*

The Free Tibet Campaign, based in London, stands for the Tibetans' right to decide their own future. It campaigns for an end to the Chinese occupation of Tibet and for the Tibetans' fundamental human rights to be respected. It is independent of all governments and is funded solely by its members and supporters.

Students for a free Tibet   *www.Tibet.org*

Universal declaration of Human Rights   *www.un.org/Overview/rights.html*

Clean Clothes Campaign   *www.cleanclothes.org*

Europe-based campaign to promote fair labor practices in the apparel industry.

Free the Children   *www.freethechildren.org*

Canadian-based international group formed to raise awareness of child labor and raise funds to create alternatives.

Alliance for Childhood   *www.allianceforchildhood.net*

The Alliance for Childhood is an international partnership working to preserve childhood as a time of special vulnerability, deserving of protection by caring, responsible adults.

Jubilee 2000   *www.jubilee2000uk.org*

Third world debt forgiveness.

Global Exchange   *www.globalexchange.org*

Anti-Slavery International   *www.antislavery.org*

Human Rights Watch   *www.hrw.org*

International Labor Organization   *www.ilo.org*

The Campaign Against Arms Trade   *www.caat.org.uk*

DEVELOPMENT

3

> Go where people sleep and see if they are safe

MYTH:

Globalization will end world hunger

REALITY:

The globalization of agriculture fails to address the world's hunger crisis. In fact it makes it worse. During the past two decades, the total amount of food in the world has increased, but so has hunger.

The main problem is that globalization of food production pushes small, self-reliant farmers off their lands and replaces them with large chemical and machine-intensive corporate farms. It does not emphasize food for hungry local communities. Instead, it encourages exports resulting in monocultures – a single crop grown over thousands of acres. These crops are usually luxury items cultivated for export and are notoriously vulnerable to insect blights and bad weather, and cause soil infertility.

Global biotechnology companies claim they have the answer to world hunger. But biotech production does nothing to solve local hunger problems. Does anyone believe that the invention of biotech plants whose seeds are sterile – forcing farmers to buy new seeds every year – has anything to do with stopping hunger? The biotech industry's goal is not to feed the hungry, only to feed itself.

A recent United Nations study confirms that the world already has enough food. The problem is one of distribution. Global trade rules put food production and distribution in the hands of agribusiness giants, supplanting the traditional system of local production for local consumption.

The world is producing the wrong kind of food, by a process that leaves millions of people landless, homeless, cashless, and unable to feed themselves.

Fair Trade - The Real Bottom Line

Anita: If trade undermines life, narrows it or impoverishes it, then it can destroy the world. If it enhances life, then it can better the world.

Anita Roddick Fair Trade. The words speak for themselves: fair means "respectful" and "honorable," trade means "barter" and "interchange." But it has begun to occur to me that there are people who don't see fair trade in quite the same way. In the USA, protectionists on the Right are invoking fair trade as an appetizer for isolationism. Where is the concept of "respectful interchange" in that?

My own experience of fair trade has been vastly different and – hopefully – much more encouraging.

It probably started as long ago as my helping my mother in her café after school and at weekends. Working there taught me that business wasn't a financial science. First and foremost, it was about an exchange, about buying and selling. My mother's bottom line was truth to her values. It meant bringing your heart and your humanity to work. I learned at an early age that these are as essential for business as they are for life.

When I look back now, I can see that my mother's café also embodied the new model of business whose slow, difficult emergence we've been tracking over the past few decades. This new model is looking for a bottom line other than price and profit. Does such a thing exist? It's scarcely a new question – John Ruskin was debating the same thing in the 19th century – but it has become one of the central issues of our new century. That's because business itself is now the most powerful force for change in the world today, richer and faster by far than most governments. And what is it doing with this power? It is using free trade, the most powerful weapon at its disposal, to tighten its grip on the globe.

I've heard free trade apologists argue that living and working conditions are likely to be worst when foreign investment is lowest, but even they concede this is not the case with the garment and footwear industries. The plain fact is that a number of basic human rights have been compromised by the fluctuations in the international labor market that globalization has fostered.

My own company's commitment to the protection of human rights has always been a non-negotiable part of the corporate DNA. It seems absolutely fundamental to me that our freedom to do business rests on other, more profound freedoms. The response, the interchange, is the essence of trading. That's why the idea of partnering has always been so appealing to me. And that's why The Body Shop has been putting resources into building a model of "community trade" that points to an alternative. Our emphasis is on supporting small-scale economic initiatives wherever we go, keeping communities vital. We now have 40 such initiatives in 26 countries around the world. We are concerned about quality in trade, not just quantity. That means supporting black family farms in America, or building a new fiber economy,or supporting new ecological designers, or teaching our employees community organizing.

It means Mexico, where, in the Mesquital Valley, north of Mexico City, the women of the Nanhu Indian tribe have been using ancient techniques perfected by the Aztecs to make body scrubs from the fibers of the maguey cactus. Indigenous women, who 10 years ago would find it difficult to leave their remote villages, have formed themselves into an association to strengthen their communities and work towards making a sustainable living. For 10 years, with the help of NGOs, they have exported their exquisite handicrafts to The Body Shop in an attempt to avoid becoming "wet backs" like so many of their family who risk their lives as illegal immigrants in the USA. The USA, where the cheap labor of thousands of such "invisible" hands, subsidizes the economy of the most powerful nation on earth.

Thanks to efforts by The Body Shop, NGOs, and the Mexico government's Solidaridad program, the women are making a sustainable living – even if it's still very tough.

Mexico, where globalization brought NAFTA, the North American Free Trade Agreement, which promised wealth and prosperity through the expansion of "free" trade but where thousands of indigenous people, like the Nahnu women we trade with, are still deprived of their most basic human rights. Mexico, where the demand for a voice for the disenfranchised indigenous population was brought into dramatic relief by the march of the guerrilla leader subcomandante Marcos on the capital city in March 2001, having eluded the might of the Mexican army for 17 years in the jungle of Chiapas. The same Chiapas where Fair Trade organizations like Twin Trading and Café Direct are also trading with coffee farmers to offer a dignified alternative to the type of "freedom" à la NAFTA.

The war that subcomandante Marcos has led in Chiapas for the last 17 years is being fought by small producers on many fronts and in many different ways all over the world. Far from bringing freedom, globalization continues to tighten the yoke of domination on the world's poor. The freedom that comes with globalization is freedom for the rich and powerful nations to further exploit and further marginalize those at the bottom of the social ladder. It is precisely these people that I am interested in working with in their struggle to take control over their own destinies. Every single one of the groups in our Community Trade program is waging this war and I believe that trade which is fair, trade that is free from exploitation, trade that brings dignity rather than dehumanizing, can play an important role in winning this war.

And women are demonstrating time and time again that they are powerful adversaries in this war. In the North East of Brazil they took on the large landowners in their struggle to gain access to the fruits of the wild-growing babassu palm. They stood up to the hired gunmen who tried to expel them from the forest as they demanded their right to something they considered a gift from God. They waged war for ten years to gain their "free babassu" because it provides them with their only means of subsistence, it is their currency for purchasing the basic food stuffs they can not grow on their tiny land-holdings. Many lives were lost in that war, but they won and now their right to the fruits of the forest is written in legislation which prevents land barons from chopping down trees. The women see themselves as the guardians of the forest. They now form part of a powerful women's movement and part of a cooperative which has been converting the babassu nuts into oil and selling to The Body Shop since 1994. The power of their movement is conveyed in these lines from the hymn to the babassu breaker:

"A woman on her feet ceases to be so scared, Be courageous, take my hand, We will struggle together with courage and with love, For the government to recognize this, our profession."

The women gained their "free babassu" and have gone some way to the recognition they demand but globalization threatened their livelihoods when the import of cheap, Malaysian palm oil into Brazil took the bottom out of the national market in babassu oil. Thanks to the trade with The Body Shop, the cooperative was able to ride the wave until the market made a modest recovery. The cooperative is now recognized as a force to be reckoned with and can be found at the same table with the major exporters of Maranhao State.

On another frontier, peasant farmers in Nicaragua have demonstrated the power of strong, community-based organization in their struggle to survive the perennial fluctuations of the commodity market in sesame seed. The same combative spirit that led to the triumph of the Sandinista revolution in the 1980s continues to this day as the battle for justice is played out through their small cooperative of sesame seed farmers. In their case, a hand-operated oil press and simple mathematics provided the tools which allowed them to build their business since they first started trading with us with less than two tonnes of oil in 1993. We commissioned the services of a consultant to carry out a careful examination of the costs of production of sesame oil. In this way, we were able to fix a guaranteed, fair price which allows the farmers to know what the return on their labor and investment will be before they go into seed production. The fair price has also allowed the cooperative to build its capital and thus provide essential credit to those who no bank will recognize as creditworthy. The cooperative shop, which provides basic foodstuffs at real prices, acts as a price moderator in their small, remote town where other traders would attempt extorsion. It allows the cooperative to support the acupuncture clinic which runs in the back of the shop to provide a much sought-after service to those who have no access to health care. The cooperative has been able to up-grade its technology and now provides us with over 70 tonnes of excellent sesame oil.

It means Ghana where, in Tamale in the north, we have been sourcing shea butter from a cooperative made up of women from 13 villages. Trade has changed the status of women in these communities. Because they now have a livelihood, they can pay for books and school uniforms for their children. They can call on a health worker when they're ill or a midwife when they're pregnant. Young girls who would once have automatically been put out to work can now get an education.

As the daughter of one of the women members of the shea butter group put it: "I nearly stopped schooling because my mother could no longer support me. Meanwhile my father was not around and my uncle too did not have money. I used to stay in the house crying whenever my friends were going to school and my mother would join me to cry. This made me feel very empty and sorry for myself and my mother. But as soon as she joined the shea butter extraction group, we have rediscovered our joy and happiness as I now attend school without any interruptions."

With each community trade initiative, we have had to adapt to the culture, the capabilities, and the limitations of our partners. As they learn, so do we. The resulting relationships are intimate and personal in a way that is the opposite of the global market syndrome, which is all about distance, impersonality, and the movement of capital regardless of human consequence. One of the strong points of our community trade program is that it has rekindled the primal connection between producer and buyer, between origin and destination.

If trade undermines life, narrows it or impoverishes it, then it can destroy the world. If it enhances life, then it can better the world. And, as John Ruskin wrote over a hundred years ago: "There is no wealth but life." That's the real bottom line.

Anita Roddick

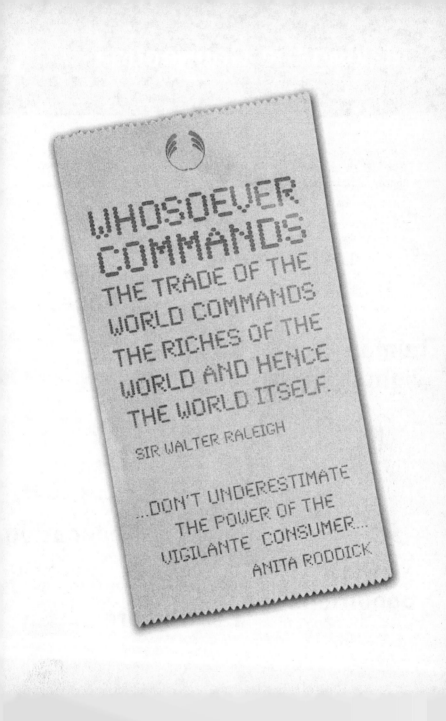

WHOSOEVER
COMMANDS
THE TRADE OF THE
WORLD COMMANDS
THE RICHES OF THE
WORLD AND HENCE
THE WORLD ITSELF.

SIR WALTER RALEIGH

...DON'T UNDERESTIMATE
THE POWER OF THE
VIGILANTE CONSUMER...

ANITA RODDICK

Wherever you are in the world, buying a fairly traded product contributes directly to the community that produces it.

environment

fair wages

human rights

education

work conditions

health care

Anita: There's always a great deal of rhetoric about how we need to race all the faster for economic "growth" because it will help the poorest people on earth. In practice, of course, the poorest people on earth often just get brushed aside in the rush – as I discovered for myself the more we got involved in the plight of the Ogoni people in the Niger Delta, swept aside by the discovery of oil where they live by Shell in 1958. Unfortunately, our campaign failed to prevent the murder of Ken Saro-Wiwa by the Nigerian government, but it did at least put the Ogoni people on the map. All over the world, in the darker corners where the media never goes, there are other people in just the same predicament. Two of the women I admire most on the planet – Helena Norberg-Hodge and Vandana Shiva – have done more than anybody else to give them a voice ...

INDIA

Vandana Shiva I was recently visiting Bhatinda in Punjab because of an epidemic of farmers' suicides. Punjab used to be the most prosperous agricultural region in India. Today, every farmer is in debt and despair. Vast stretches of land have become waterlogged desert. And, as an old farmer pointed out, even the trees have stopped bearing fruit because heavy use of pesticides has killed the pollinators – the bees and butterflies.

And Punjab is not alone in experiencing this ecological and social disaster. Last year I was in Warangal, Andhra Pradesh, where farmers have also been committing suicide. Farmers who traditionally grew pulses and millets and paddy have been lured by seed companies to buy hybrid cotton seeds referred to as "white gold," which were supposed to make them millionaires. Instead they became paupers.

Their native seeds have been displaced with new hybrids which cannot be saved and need to be purchased every year at a high cost. Hybrids are also very vulnerable to pest attacks. Spending on pesticides in Warangal has increased 2,000 percent from $2.5 million in the 1980s to £50 million in 1997. Now farmers are consuming the same pesticides as a way of killing themselves so that they can escape permanently from unpayable debt.

The corporations are now trying to introduce genetically engineered seed, which will further increase costs and ecological risks. That is why farmers like Malla Reddy of the Andhra Pradesh Farmers' Union had uprooted Monsanto's genetically engineered Bollgard cotton in Warangal.

On March 27, 25-year-old Betavati Ratan took his life because he could not pay back debts for drilling a deep tube well on his two-acre farm. The wells are now dry, as are the wells in Gujarat and Rajasthan where more than 50 million people face a water famine. The drought is not a "natural disaster." It is man-made. It is the result of mining of scarce ground water in arid regions to grow thirsty cash crops for export instead of water-prudent food crops for local needs.

Who really feeds the world? My answer is very different from that given by most people. It is women and small farmers working with biodiversity who are the primary food providers in the third world and, contrary to the dominant assumption, their diverse small farm systems are more productive than industrial monocultures.

The rich diversity and sustainable systems of food production have been destroyed in the name of increasing food production. But with the destruction of diversity, rich sources of nutrition disappear. When measured in terms of nutrition per acre, and from the perspective of biodiversity, the so-called "high yields" of industrial agriculture do not imply more production of food and nutrition.

Yield usually refers to production per unit area of a single crop. Output refers to the total production of diverse crops and products. Planting only one crop in the entire field as a monoculture will, of course, increase its individual yield. Planting multiple crops in a mixture will have low yields of individual crops, but will have high total output of food. Yields have been defined in such a way as to make the food production on small farms, by small farmers, disappear.

This hides the production by millions of women farmers in the third world – farmers like those in my native Himalaya who fought against logging in the Chipko movement, who in their terraced fields grow Jhangora (barnyard millet), Marsha (amaranth), Tur (pigeon pea), Urad (black gram), Gahat (horse gram), soy bean (glycine max), Bhat (glycine soya), Rayans (rice bean), Swanta (cow pea), Koda (finger millet). Diverse productivity is higher than monoculture productivity. I call this blindness to the high productivity of diversity a "monoculture of the mind," which creates monocultures in our fields.

The Mayan peasants in the Chiapas are characterized as unproductive because they produce only two tons of corn per acre. But the overall food output is 20 tons per acre when the diversity of their beans and squashes, their vegetables and fruit trees is taken into account. In Java, small farmers cultivate 607 species in their home gardens. In sub-saharan Africa, women cultivate as many as 120 different plants in the spaces left alongside the cash crops, and this is the main source of household food security.

A single home garden in Thailand has more than 230 species, and African home gardens have more than 50 species of tree. Rural families in the Congo eat leaves from more than 50 different species of tree.

A study in eastern Nigeria found that home gardens occupying only two percent of a household's farmland accounted for half the farm's total output. Similarly, home gardens in Indonesia are estimated to provide more than 20 percent of household income and 40 percent of domestic food supplies.

Research done by the UN's Food and Agriculture Organization has shown that small biodiverse farms can produce thousands of times more food than large, industrial monocultures.

And diversity is the best strategy for preventing drought and desertification. What the world needs to feed a growing population sustainably is biodiversity intensification, not chemical intensification or genetic engineering. While women and small peasants feed the world through biodiversity, we are repeatedly told that without genetic engineering and globalization of agriculture the world will starve. In spite of all empirical evidence showing that genetic engineering does not produce more food and in fact often leads to a yield decline, it is constantly promoted as the only alternative available for feeding the hungry.

That is why I ask: who feeds the world? This deliberate blindness to diversity, the blindness to nature's production, production by women, production by third world farmers, allows destruction and appropriation to be projected as creation.

Take the case of the much-flaunted "golden rice" or genetically engineered vitamin A rice as a cure for blindness. It is assumed that without genetic engineering we cannot remove vitamin A deficiency. Yet nature gives us abundant and diverse sources of vitamin A. If rice were not polished, rice itself would provide vitamin A. If herbicides were not sprayed on our wheat fields, we would have bathua, amaranth, mustard leaves as delicious and nutritious greens.

Women in Bengal use more than 150 plants as greens. But the myth of creation presents biotechnologists as the creators of vitamin A, negating nature's diverse gifts and women's knowledge of how to use this diversity to feed their children and families. The most efficient means of rendering the destruction of nature, local economies, and small autonomous producers is by rendering their production invisible.

Farmers everywhere are being paid a fraction of what they received for the same commodity a decade ago. In the US, wheat prices dropped from $5.75 to $2.43, soya bean prices dropped from $8.40 to $4.29, and corn prices dropped from $4.43 to $1.72 a bushel. In India, from 1999 to 2000, prices for coffee dropped from Rs.60 to Rs.18 per kg and prices of oilseeds declined by more than 30 percent.

While farmers earn less, consumers, especially in poor countries, pay more. In India, food prices have doubled between 1999 and 2000, and consumption of food grains has dropped by 12 percent in rural areas, increasing the food deprivation of those already malnourished, pushing up mortality rates. Increased economic growth through global commerce is based on pseudo surpluses. More food is being traded while the poor are consuming less. When growth increases poverty, when real production becomes a negative economy, and speculators are defined as "wealth creators," something has gone wrong with the concepts and categories of wealth and wealth creation.

According to the McKinsey corporation, American food giants recognize that Indian agro-business has lots of room to grow, especially in food processing. India processes a minuscule one percent of the food it grows compared with 70 percent for the US, Brazil, and the Philippines. It is not that we Indians eat our food raw. Global consultants fail to see the 99 percent food processing done by women at household level, or by small cottage industry, because it is not controlled by global agribusiness: 99 percent of India's agro-processing has been intentionally kept at the household level.

Now, under the pressure of globalization, things are changing. Pseudo hygiene laws that shut down the food economy based on small-scale local processing under community control are part of the arsenal of global agribusiness for establishing market monopolies through force and coercion, not competition.

In August 1998, small-scale local processing of edible oil was banned in India through a "packaging order" which made sale of open oil illegal and required all oil to be packed in plastic or aluminium. This shut down tiny "ghanis" or cold-pressed mills. It destroyed the market for our diverse oilseeds – mustard, linseed, sesame, groundnut, and coconut.

The take-over of the edible oil industry has affected 10 million livelihoods. The take-over of "atta" or flour by packaged branded flour will cost 100 million livelihoods. These millions are being pushed into new poverty. The forced use of packaging will increase the environmental burden of millions of tonnes of plastic and aluminium. The globalization of the food system is destroying the diversity of local food cultures and local food economies. A global monoculture is being forced on people by defining everything that is fresh, local, and handmade as a health hazard. Human hands are being defined as the worst contaminants, and work for human hands is being outlawed, to be replaced by machines and chemicals bought from global corporations.

As humans travel further down the road to non-sustainability, they become intolerant of other species and blind to their vital role in our survival. In 1992, when Indian farmers destroyed Cargill's seed plant in Bellary, Karnataka, as a protest against seed failure, the Cargill chief executive said: "We bring Indian farmers smart technologies which prevent bees from usurping the pollen."

When I was participating in the United Nations Biosafety Negotiations, Monsanto circulated literature to defend its Roundup herbicide-resistant crops on grounds that they prevent "weeds from stealing the sunshine." But what Monsanto calls weeds are the green fields that provide vitamin A rice and prevent blindness in children and anaemia in women. A world-view that defines pollination as "theft by bees" and claims that biodiversity "steals" sunshine is a world-view which itself aims at stealing nature's harvest by replacing open, pollinated varieties with hybrids and sterile seeds, and at destroying biodiverse flora with herbicides such as Monsanto's Roundup. The threat posed to the Monarch butterfly by genetically engineered crops is just one example of the ecological poverty created by the new biotechnologies. As butterflies and bees disappear, production is undermined. As biodiversity disappears, with it go sources of nutrition and food.

When giant corporations view small peasants and bees as thieves, and through trade rules and new technologies seek the right to exterminate them, humanity has reached a dangerous threshold. The imperative to stamp out the smallest insect, the smallest plant, the smallest peasant comes from a deep fear – the fear of everything that is alive and free. And this deep insecurity and fear is unleashing violence against all people and all species.

Vandana Shiva is a physicist and president of the Research Foundation for Science, Technology and Ecology. She is also one of India's leading activists.

If enough **species** are extinguished,
will the **ecosystem** collapse,
and will the **extinction** of most other
species follow soon **afterward?**

The only answer anyone can give is: **possibly.**

By the time we find out however, it might be too late.
One planet, one experiment.

 E. O. Wilson

Anita: What exactly is "progress"? It can't possibly mean the same thing for each person on the face of the planet, and yet we insist on imposing a generic version of the concept in the most unsuitable circumstances – which suggests that our faith in "progress" is at best misplaced, at worst blind.

Helena Norberg-Hodge

The world, we are told, is being transformed into a "global village." Illuminated by bright neon signs, fed by McDonald's, the "global village" is said to be a place where "outmoded" cultural and religious beliefs have been consigned to history, leaving a modern world of peaceful and contented consumers: neo-Westerners, in fact. The truth could hardly be more different.

Consider Ladakh, a remote region of broad valleys set about with peaks that rise to 20,000 feet in the trans-Himalayan region of Kashmir. When I first lived among the Ladakhis in the early 1970s, they enjoyed peace of mind. The pace of their lives was relaxed and easy. An important element in this stress-free lifestyle was the fact that they had control over their own lives. Over the last thirty years, however, I have watched as external forces have descended on the Ladakhis like an avalanche, causing massive and rapid disruption.

The process of change began in earnest in 1974, when the Indian government threw the area open to tourism. At about the same time, concerted efforts were made to develop the district. As everywhere else in the world, development in Ladakh has meant Western-style economic growth-oriented development. This process has consisted primarily of building up the so-called "infrastructure" – especially roads, and energy plants.

In the traditional culture, villagers provided for their basic needs without money. They had developed skills that enabled them to grow barley at 12,000 feet and to manage yaks and other animals at even higher elevations. People knew how to build houses with their own hands from the materials of the immediate surroundings. The only thing they actually needed from outside the region was salt, for which they traded. Then, suddenly, as part of the international economy, Ladakhis found themselves ever more dependent – even for vital needs – on a system that is controlled by faraway forces.

The process has been extremely complex and involves the systemic transformation of a whole way of life. It is very clear, however, that the pull to the center is to a great extent the result of deliberate planning: the West's addiction to economic growth puts pressure on others to develop, and in order to create the conditions for development, governments expend vast resources to restructure society. Everywhere, the underlying infrastructure – from centralized energy production, to Western, urbanizing education – is essentially the same. And so, too, are the consequent problems.

In the traditional economy, Ladakhis knew that they had to depend on other people, and they took care of them. But in the new economic system, the distance between people has increased so that it now appears that you no longer need one another. The fabric of local interdependence is disintegrating, and so too are the traditional levels of tolerance and cooperation.

As mutual aid is replaced by dependence on external markets, people begin to feel powerless to make decisions in their own lives. At all levels, a feeling of disempowerment has afflicted Ladakhi society. In the traditional village, repairing irrigation canals was a task shared by the whole community. As soon as a channel developed a leak, groups of people would start working away with shovels patching it up. Now, such work is seen as the government's responsibility – a channel is left to leak until someone else fixes it.

As they lose the sense of security and identity that springs from long-lasting connections to other people and the land, Ladakhis are starting to be plagued by self-doubt. At the same time, tourism and the media are presenting a new image of who they should be. They are meant to lead an essentially Western lifestyle: eating dinner at a dining table, driving a car, using a washing machine. The images are telling them to be different, to be better than they are.

Ironically, then, modernization – so often associated with the defense of individualism – has eroded Ladakhis' sense of personal identity. As people become self-conscious and insecure, they feel under pressure to conform, to live up to the new, idealized images. By contrast, in the traditional village, where everyone wore the same clothes and looked superficially similar, there seemed to be more freedom to relax and be who you really were. As part of a close-knit community, people felt secure enough to be themselves.

The previously outgoing and confident women of Ladakh have also become increasingly insecure about their lives, and about their appearance in particular. Despite their new dominant role, men also suffer. As a result of the breakdown of family and community ties, they are deprived of contact with children. As youngsters, the new macho image prevents them from showing any affection, while in later life as fathers their work keeps them away from home.

Competition for the scarce jobs available, and for political representation within the new centralized structures, increasingly divides Ladakhis. Ethnic and religious differences have begun to take on a political dimension, causing bitterness and enmity on a scale hitherto unknown.

This new rivalry is one of the most dramatic and disturbing developments I have seen in Ladakh. Over the space of just a few years, growing competition culminated in actual violence. The first time I noticed any signs of group tension was in 1986, when I heard Ladakhi friends starting to define people according to whether they were Muslim or Buddhist. And then, in the summer of 1989, fighting broke out between the two groups. Major disturbances in Leh bazaar resulted in four people being shot dead by police – much of Ladakh was placed under curfew. Prior to this, there had not been a fight in living memory. Indeed, when I had asked a friend how everyone managed to live so peacefully together, he said simply, "What a funny question. We just live with each other, that's all."

Westerners often assume that ethnic and religious strife is increasing because modern democracy liberates people, allowing old prejudices and hatreds to surface. If there was peace earlier, they assume it was the result of oppression. But after more than twenty years of firsthand experience on the Indian subcontinent, I am convinced that "development" not only exacerbates existing tensions but in many cases actually creates them. Development causes artificial scarcity, which inevitably leads to greater competition, and it pressures people to conform to a standard Western model that they simply cannot emulate.

To strive for such an ideal is to reject one's own culture and roots – in effect to reject one's own identity. The resulting alienation gives rise to confusion, resentment, and anger, and lies behind much of the violence and fundamentalism in the world today. This is the simmering, chaotic reality behind the harmonious façade of the "global village."

Whenever **you** are in **doubt**, apply the following **test**: recall the **face** of the **poorest** and weakest **person** you may have **seen** and **ask** yourself if the **step** you **contemplate** is **going** to be of **any use** to them.

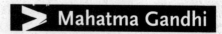 Mahatma Gandhi

The global corporatists preach a model of economic growth that rests on the flows of trade and finance between nations dominated by the giant multinationals – drugs, tobacco, oil, banking and other services. The global corporate model is premised on the concentration of power over markets, governments, mass media, patent monopolies over critical drugs and seeds, the workplace and corporate culture. All these and other power concentrates homogenize the globe and undermine democratic processes and their benefits.

Far better for countries to focus on building domestic markets through land reform, microcredit for small businesses, use of local materials for housing and renewable energy solar-style. For developing countries, it is far better for bottom-up capital formation to encourage activities that are more job intensive – generating purchasing power – than adopting highly capitalized and chemical plantation-type agribusiness with destructive technologies.

Rice - The story of Basmati Rice

Anita: All shoplifters will be prosecuted!

INDIA

Vandana Shiva A US-based company has been granted a patent for basmati rice lines and grains. Basmati, neem, pepper, bitter gourd, turmeric, made by my mother and grandmother... every aspect of the innovation embodied in our indigenous food and medicinal systems is now being pirated and patented. The knowledge of the poor is being converted into the property of global corporations, creating a situation where the poor will have to pay for the seeds and medicines they have evolved and have used to meet their needs for nutrition and health care.

Such false claims to creation are now the global norm, with the Trade Related Intellectual Property Rights Agreement of the WTO forcing countries to introduce regimes that allow patenting of life forms and indigenous knowledge. Humans do not create life when they manipulate it. The company claims that it has made "an instant invention of a novel rice line," or the Roslin Institute's claim that Ian Wilmut "created" Dolly denies the creativity of nature, the self-organizational capacity of life forms, and the prior innovation of third world communities.

When patents are granted for seeds and plants, as in the case of basmati, theft is defined as creation, and saving and sharing seed is defined as theft of intellectual property. Corporations which have broad patents on crops such as cotton, soya bean, and mustard are suing farmers for seed-saving and hiring detective agencies to find out if farmers have saved seed or shared it with neighbors.

Vandana Shiva

Anita: The status quo takes no notice of people on the margins — they must take their future into their own hands.

MEXICO

Ya basta – "enough is enough" – has become the catch phrase of an extraordinary movement in the southernmost state of Mexico. They call themselves the Zapatista Army of National Liberation. They fit no current political mold of what a revolution, or a revolutionary movement, should look like. The Right have tried to apply the same old labels – subversives, guerrillas, terrorists – but remain unconvincing. The Left have attempted to co-opt them by calling them Marxists, Leninists, Trotskyites, anarchists and the like, but have equally failed.

The Zapatista revolution, unlike almost all others, doesn't aim to replace state power, either by using guns or the ballot box. Instead, the Zapatistas say: "We want a world in which there are many worlds, a world in which our world, and the worlds of others will fit: a world in which we are heard, but as one of many voices."

What makes the Zapatista rebellion so interesting is that it is primarily an uprising by indigenous peoples. They are not one people, but rather several, each with different languages and customs. Harry Cleaver, an academic and activist with a close interest in the Zapatistas says: "In a very real sense, the Zapatista movement emerged as a tentative and transitory solution to precisely the problem which confronts us everywhere: how to link up a diverse array of linguistically and culturally distinct peoples and their struggles, despite and beyond those distinctions, how to weave a variety of struggles into one struggle that never loses its multiplicity."

The question of linking up diverse struggles is very much what this book is about.

Brothers and Sisters:

On this 21st of March of 2000, in which the birth of Benito Jua'rez is celebrated, according to the official calendar, he who stated some words which have not, to date, been carried out by the Mexican Government, the Federal and the State. What Benito Jua'rez said was "RESPECT FOR THE RIGHTS OF OTHERS IS PEACE." You might ask why we are saying this, it is for the following:

1. We are almost imprisoned in our communities in this Selva-Border region, by the incredible number of soldiers and various kinds of police that there are in the region. We cannot move about freely in order to carry out our daily activities on our plots, without fear that they will take away our tools, such as machetes, axes, chain saws, and others.

2. Since the conflict arose in 1994, we have been subjected to the attack of the low intensity war, which is how we view the fact that, through the Moscamed program which fights the Mediterranean fly (the fruit fly), using this as an excuse, they have fumigated our plots planted with coffee, maize, beans, pineapple, bananas, and other fruits and vegetables, with Malathion (we are well aware, through the training we have received, and through what our companero and companera campesinos have shared with us, that the use of this liquid is prohibited, because it is considered to be one of the most dangerous poisons to humans).

3. We consider this to be part of the aggression of the war of extermination against the indigenous peoples being waged by powerful countries, who want to efficiently impose neo-liberalism, we consider this to be so because the liquid has caused:

- Acceleration of the destruction of the region's ecological equilibrium.

- A decrease in the production of coffee crops, beans, maize, fruit trees, and shade trees, since the crops are easily losing their leaves, flowers, and tender fruit.

- A worsening of malnutrition and health of the boys and girls, and of the residents in general, since, with the decrease in production, the consumption of vegetables and fruits decreases, and, in general, the provision of well-being in clothing, shoes, and the education of our boys and girls, because, by not harvesting the same amount of products such as coffee, family income decreases.

- Contamination of the water and air, since they are throwing Malathion in plastic bags which then break, and the poison falls in the water and the air which we breathe, and health is being affected by consuming contaminated water.

Because of the foregoing, we consider these actions to be violations of the Indigenous Human Rights. These articles refer to the rights which all of us, as Indian peoples, have, in the lands which we have under our care, where we are living, working, playing, and loving.

4 We have made our voice and opinions known many times, and the government does not hear, does not see, does not smell, it does not perceive the flavors of such diverse words, our words.

Moscamed is low intensity chemical war
Denuncia from the Tierra y Libertad Autonomous
Municipality and Civil Society of the Selva-Border Region

Subcommander Marcos' letter to the people of the USA

Anita: Insurgent Subcommander Marcos is the charismatic mystery man at the head of the Zapatistas. Although not Mayan himself, he has dedicated himself to helping the indigenous people in the jungles and mountains of Chiapas. His regular communiqués through the EZLN's website Ya Basta! have mobilized global opinion on behalf of the Zapatistas. That is due in part to Marcos' compelling writing style, which colors him as a magic realist in the grand Central American literary tradition. He has called the Zapatista cause "a struggle for human dignity, a struggle to be better." Originally a "mestizo," a city boy, Marcos has put himself on the front line to protect and preserve irreplaceable indigenous traditions that are being destroyed by "progress." As he himself has said, his time with the Indians has converted him from teacher to student, "taught him how to listen and to try to understand what is behind words..."

MEXICO

The US government has been wrong more than once in regards to its foreign policy. When this has occurred it is due to the fact it is making a mistake as to the man it ought to be backing up. History is not lacking in this type of example. In the first half of this decade, the US government made a mistake backing Carlos Salinas de Gortari. It made a mistake signing a Nafta which lacked a majority support from the North American people and which meant an order of summary execution against the Mexican Indigenous people. On the dawn of 1994 we rose up in arms. We rose up not seeking power, not responding to a foreign order. We rose up to say "here we are." The Mexican government, our government, had forgotten us and was ready to perpetrate a genocide without bullets or bombs, it was ready to annihilate us with the quiet death of sickness, of misery, of oblivion. The US government became the accomplice of the Mexican government in this genocide.

With the signing of Nafta, the US government acted as guarantor of and gave its blessing to the murder of millions of Mexicans. Did the people of the US know this? Did it know that its government was signing accords of massive extermination in Mexico? Did the people of the US know that their government was backing a criminal? That man is gone. We remained. Our demands had not been solved and our arms kept saying "here we are" to the new government, to the people of Mexico, to the people and governments of the world.

We waited patiently for the new government to listen to us and pay attention to us. But, within the dark circles of US power someone decided that we, the insurgent Indigenous people of the Mexican South East, were the worst threat to the United States of America. From the darkness came the order: finish them up!

They put a price on our brown skin, on our culture, on our word, because, above all they put a price on our uprising. The US government decided, once more, to back a man, someone who continues with the politics of deceit of his predecessor, someone who denies the people of Mexico democracy, freedom, and justice. Millions of dollars were lent to that man and his government. Without the approval of the American people, an enormous loan, without precedent in history, was granted to the Mexican government. Not to improve the living conditions of the people, not for the democratization of the country's political life, not for the economic reactivation promoting factories and productive projects. This money is for speculation, for corruption, for simulation, for the annihilation of a group of rebels, Indians for the most part, poorly armed, poorly nourished, ill-equipped, but very dignified, very rebellious, and very human.

So much money to finance deceit can only be explained by fear. But, what does the US government fear? Truth? That the North American people realize that their money is helping to back the oldest dictatorship in the modern world? That the North American people realize that their taxes pay for the persecution and death of the Mexican Indian population? What is the North American people afraid of? Ought the people of North America fear our wooden rifles, our bare feet, our exhausted bodies, our language, our culture? Ought the North American people fear our scream in demand of democracy, liberty, and justice? Aren't these three truths the foundation which brought forth the birth of the United States of America? Aren't democracy, liberty, and justice rights that belong to all human beings?

Americans: the attacks against the Mexican nation brought about by political US personalities have been big and numerous. In their analysis they point out the awkwardness and corruption of the Mexican government (an awkwardness and corruption which have increased and are maintained under the shadow of the US government's support) and they identify them with an entire people who take shelter under the Mexican flag. They are wrong.

Mexico is not a government. Mexico is a nation which aspires to be sovereign and independent, and in order to be that must liberate itself from a dictatorship and raise on its soil the universal flag of democracy, liberty, and justice. Fermenting racism, fear, and insecurity, the great personalities of US politics offer economic support to the Mexican government so that it controls by violent means the discontent against the economic situation. They offer to multiply the absurd walls with which they pretend to put a stop to the search for life which drives millions of Mexicans to cross the northern border.

The best wall against massive immigration to the US is a free, just, and democratic regime in Mexico. If Mexicans could find in their own land what now is denied them, they would not be forced to look for work in other countries. By supporting the dictatorship of the state party system in Mexico, whatever the name of the man or the party, the North American people are supporting an uncertain and anguishing future. By supporting the people of Mexico in their aspirations for democracy, liberty, and justice, the North American people honor their history... and their human condition.

Health and long life to the people of the United States of America.

From the Mexican South East Insurgent
Subcommander Marcos
Mexico, September 13, 1995

Anita: Throughout my time at The Body Shop we have been struggling to find new ways of trading directly with communities, so that the benefits can really spread to local people, and so that the power stays with them. If it wasn't handmade paper from the Kathmandu Valley, it was Brazil nuts from the Kayapo. Deciding whether to trade or not to trade is always difficult, but sometimes it seems to me really pretty easy. Should we be trading with disreputable regimes like the one in Burma? That was what the respected journalist John Pilger asked Aung San Suu Kyi.

Aung San Suu Kyi and John Pilger

Aung San Suu Kyi – Burma's elected leader – was born in 1945, the daughter of Burma's national hero Aung San. She was two years old when he was assassinated, just before Burma gained the independence to which he had dedicated his life. After her education in Rangoon, Delhi, and Oxford, she worked for the United Nations in New York and Bhutan. She married an Englishman and spent several years raising a family in England. Then in 1988 she returned to Burma to care for her dying mother. Her return coincided with the outbreak of a spontaneous revolt against 26 years of political repression and economic decline. Suu Kyi quickly emerged as the most effective and articulate leader of the movement and the party she founded, the National League for Democracy, went on to win a colossal electoral victory in 1990. But the military junta refused to transfer power as it had promised and kept her under house-arrest in Rangoon. From her home she now organizes weekly political meetings – but she is as much at risk as any other citizen in Burma and the regime still finds ways of restricting her movement and her contacts with the outside world.

John Pilger: How can you reclaim the democracy that you won at the ballot box from the uncompromising and brutal power that confronts you?

Aung San Suu Kyi: We are not the first people to have had to face an uncompromising, brutal power in the quest for freedom and basic human rights. I think we have to depend chiefly on the will of our own people for democracy. In Buddhism, we are taught the four basic ingredients for success: first you must have the will to want it; then you must have the right kind of attitude; then you must have perseverance; and then you must have wisdom. So we hope to combine these four. The will of the people for democracy is there and many of us have the right kind of spirit or attitude. A number of our people have shown tremendous perseverance; and I hope we'll acquire wisdom as we go along the way...

JP: Is it not fair to describe your release from house-arrest as an entirely cynical decision by the regime to give itself a human face in order to encourage foreign investment?

SK: I think perhaps they also miscalculated the situation. They may have calculated that the National League for Democracy was a spent force and that releasing me was not going to make any difference...

JP: Should foreign investors come?

SK: I do not think they should come yet – and I am speaking for them as well as for the people of Burma. From the point of view of the people of Burma, there is hardly any investment coming in now that will provide employment and better standards of living for those who really need help. From the point of view of the investors, the basic structures necessary for sustained economic growth do not yet exist in Burma. Investing now may go against economic growth because it may make the authorities think that the half-measures they have taken are sufficient... but they are not and this will lead to social and economic problems which will work against the interests of the investors themselves.

JP: What do you say to foreign politicians who say that Burma is heading towards democracy and therefore investment is justifiable?

SK: Investment is not justifiable now. But I am convinced that Burma is heading towards democracy because it's what the people want – and in spite of investment, not because of it.

JP: A lot of Western politicians say that through commercial contacts with democratic nations the Burmese people will gain experience of democratic principles.

SK: Not in the least. The so-called "open-market economy" is only open to some. Commercial contacts are certainly not going to help Burmese people get democratic ideas. New investments help a small elite get richer. I would have thought that this would work against the very idea of democracy because the gap between rich and poor is growing all the time.

JP: What can people around the world do to help?

SK: First, think about the situation in Burma. Then I would ask them to study the UN General Assembly Resolution on Burma and to help implement it. It's a good resolution: it calls for the early and full restoration of democracy, for the acknowledgement of the will of the people in the 1990 elections, and for the full participation of the people in the political life of Burma. And, of course, it calls for the release of political prisoners and observation of basic human rights.

Aung San Suu Kyi and John Pilger

Anita: Doing business in Burma means getting into bed with a vicious military regime that is also profiting from the heroin trade.

Burma, renamed Myanmar by the current government, has for years been criticized as a military dictatorship. The people of Burma have no rights. Efforts to speak out against the dictatorship are crushed. Torture and rape are commonly used by the military as a tool of social control. Forced labor is a daily occurrence and children are regularly forced to act as porters for the military. Wages are as low as 4 cents an hour for a 45-hour workweek or just $8 a month. Companies producing there count on the regime's military power to crush any labor uprisings or efforts to speak out against the dictatorship. There are more than 1,000 political prisoners suffering in Burmese jails.

The International Labor Organization (ILO) – a tripartite agency of the United Nations that represents business, labor and government equally – suspended Burma's voting rights as a sanction for its continued practice of forced labor. And in an action unprecedented in the ILO's 80-year history, the organization censured Burma in early June 2000 for forced labor practices and encouraged national governments to apply economic sanctions, including trade and investment restrictions on Burma.

Foreign companies are not allowed to operate independently in Burma, but are required to be in joint ventures with the military government. Apparel and textile firms in Burma are part-owned and controlled by the Burmese military government and the military itself. A portion of money earned from garment exports to the US goes directly to the regime and is used to purchase weapons to repress the people of Burma.

Information provided by the Free Burma Coalition, Trillium Asset Management in Boston, the Burma Project, Canadian Friends of Burma, New Economy Communications and others.

From nlcnet.org (Charlie Kernaghan)
Source: *New Internationalist*

"We do not **feel** that we can **adequately** apply our **human rights standards** and do **business** in **Burma**."

 Reebok

"Under current **circumstances**, it is **not possible** to do **business** in **Myanmar** without directly **supporting** the **military government** and its **pervasive violations** of **human rights**."

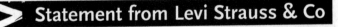 Statement from Levi Strauss & Co

after the company pulled production out of Burma

Premier Oil is a UK-based oil exploration and extraction company with stakes in North Sea oilfields and Burma. Premier Oil's consortium has a 20-year contract to sell oil to the Electricity Generating Authority of Thailand. This is being extracted from the Yetagun block in the Gulf of Martaban, then pumped across Burma through a new pipeline.

Though Premier Oil insists their presence in the region has brought schools and roads to the region, it is a fact that the pipeline has caused upheaval for millions of people, including the estimated 8 to 10 million, among them women and children, forced by Burma's military regime to work on construction. And however good Premier Oil's intentions may be, it is another fact that more than $110 million from the consortium will go the state-owned oil company, thus helping to maintain a brutal regime that affects every one of the 45 million people who live in Burma.

A strong international grassroots movement of consumers, students, and corporate shareholders is striving to convince businesses to keep out of Burma. Already many companies, including PepsiCo, Heineken, Carlsberg, Macy's, Levi's, Reebok, Eddie Bauer, and others have pulled out of Burma or decided not to invest there because of consumer pressure. Others, like Apple, Motorola, and Kodak, have quit Burma in the face of selective purchasing laws that bar local governments from awarding contracts for goods, services, or construction to companies doing business in Burma.

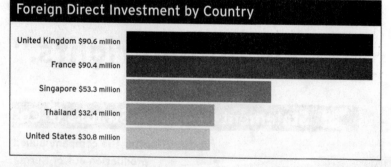

Foreign Direct Investment by Country

United Kingdom	$90.6 million
France	$90.4 million
Singapore	$53.3 million
Thailand	$32.4 million
United States	$30.8 million

Compiled from various sources by the Open Society Institute

In 1989, the Burmese military adopted a new strategy to consolidate its rule. The regime negotiated ceasefire agreements with several ethnic groups. Among the first were armies comprised of Wa and Kokang peoples that had formerly served the Communist Party of Burma and were deeply involved in heroin trafficking. The pacts allowed the United Wa State Army, the Myanmar National Democratic Alliance Army of Kokang, and others to trade freely within Burma without governmental interference. The agreements also allowed opium cultivation – the main source of income for many poor farmers – to continue for at least ten years. "As a result," the US State Department declared in its 1997 Drug Strategy Report, "these regions have become drug trafficking havens where heroin is produced and trafficked without any risk."

Burma Project

Bangkok: [Burma's] Defence Services Academy in Pyin-Oo-Lwin [Maymyu] has this year tripled its intake of officer cadets to 1,500, according to Asian intelligence sources. The reason for the increase in intake is not clear. Analysts estimate that about one-third of army battalions are under-strength and some suggest that a further build-up of forces is planned. Military strength has more than doubled from 180,000 to an estimated 400,000 since Myanmar's current regime assumed power in 1988. Military salaries increased by 500 percent on 1 April compared with a threefold rise granted to civil servants. The salary rises may be explained by the financial boost Yangon received this year as revenue began to flow from natural gas exports to Thailand.

Source: Bruce Hawke, *Jane's Defence Weekly* November 22, 2000

WDM Website

www.wdm.org.uk

The important message from the examples of people's action in this book is that we have the collective power to create a better future, if only we are sufficiently motivated to use it, and sufficiently well-organized to use it strategically. Far from feeling disempowered by the increasing intrusiveness of global institutions, we should feel that we are on the verge of winning deep changes in policies and institutions that could forever change the patterns of exploitation that have characterized our history.

The World Development Movement (WDM) was formed in 1970 as a democratic network of individuals and community action groups to win changes to the laws, policies, and institutions that are dominated by the North, in order to create opportunities for people in the South.

WDM's People before Profits campaign aims to tackle the roots of corporate power. The campaign has mobilized public action against companies that abuse the rights of stakeholders in the South. In 1997 WDM joined with banana workers to target multinationals over their victimization of union organizers, abuse of women workers, and unsafe practices that left men sterile from toxic chemicals. After a long campaign, one of the major multinationals (Del Monte) signed an agreement with trade unions to recognize the rights of workers. In 1998, WDM successfully mobilized public support for a World Health Organization agreement on tobacco marketing. In the following year WDM campaigned for a strong Biosafety Protocol. This agreement, signed in January 2000, gives governments the right to say no to genetically modified organisms.

Since the mid-1980s, WDM has campaigned to release the poorest people in the world from the burden of debt that means foreign banks, governments, and financial institutions take a large proportion of government budgets, drastically reducing available funds for basic needs.

WDM was one of the founders of the Jubilee 2000 coalition, which raised public awareness on the injustice of debt through the world's largest ever petition. But the rhetoric of politicians cannot disguise the fact that few of the world's poor have received any tangible benefit from debt relief. WDM will continue to campaign until they do, and until they have the opportunity to determine their own policies and shape their own futures.

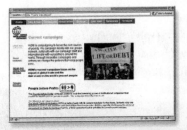

Barry Coates

1 **Join in with others to act strategically.** Join in with a campaigning organization at a local or national level, or a group of campaigners acting together. The important thing is to multiply our impact across the world.

2 **Tell others!** Friends, relatives, neighbors, the person next to you on the train (it works!)

3 **Use the democratic process.** As flawed as it sometimes is, we need our politicians to listen to us, not the corporate lobbyists. Write letters to your political representative, respond to their responses, see them in their offices, join with others locally to arrange meetings, and make sure you always vote!

4 **Get the media involved.** Write letters to the local and national papers, and join with others to get stories into the media — remember, local media are always looking for good stories.

5 **Join in events**, be good to others in the movement, act with conviction but without violence, feel good about what you're doing, and enjoy the actions you take!

6 **Be an aware consumer.** Find out about the things you buy, the holidays you take, and the services you use. Always ask for information about the conditions under which products were made – were the workers given a living wage, do they have rights, what is the impact on the environment? Ask them for evidence.

7 **Challenge the claims of companies** that they are behaving ethically – we need proof not PR.

8 **Ensure any money you have saved is invested ethically.** And make sure your pension funds are invested ethically.

9 **Buy Fair Trade** and community trade products – this is a radical alternative and a way to provide a voice for marginalized producers.

10 **Keep on doing these things.** Again and again. This is the way to build a truly global movement for change.

Barry Coates is director of the World Development Movement.

The work could be anything from stuffing envelopes in your nearest center to going abroad and helping people who need your skills. These groups do amazing work and often need help with fundraising. Give as generously as you can.

OXFAM Volunteering

www.oxfam.org

All of the Oxfams work with volunteers. If you have a few hours to spare and would like to be involved, it may be possible to work in a shop or office, helping your local Oxfam. You can join in campaigns, advocacy, and fundraising work. To find out more, please contact the Oxfam in your country of residence or your nearest Oxfam store.

From: Alliance for a Responsible, Plural and United World

www.echo.org

The International Youth Parliament, held in Sydney from October 19–28, 2000 gathered more than 240 young people from about 150 countries. This event was the fruit of an initiative of Brett Solomon, from Oxfam–Australia and co-ordinator of the Youth Workshop for Australia-Pacific. It aimed at having the participants seek youthful solutions for the challenges they face world-wide in 3 areas: "breaking the cycle of poverty," "youth in conflict," and "cultural activism." The focus of the Parliament was for young people to get new skills, to network, and to develop concrete individual and collective strategies to address the issues identified. The participants worked together to identify the issues, make proposals to address them, and draw concrete collective projects to foster social change on these issues. The projects elaborated are diverse – from developing "green" (environmentally-oriented and/or respectful) jobs to lobbying airline companies for them to show culture-sensitive videos of the destination countries during the flight, or to campaigning in support of the UN Convention on the Rights of Children.

The Parliament was also a wonderful occasion for young people to get to know one another and each other's culture: there was a real emulation during the "share your culture" sessions over lunch and many warm, funny and moving moments.

The IYP also offered for many opportunities to network, build friendships and partnerships. This is now maintained with the help of Internet discussion lists that make ongoing work and follow-up easier. The diversity and complementarity of skills, experiences, fields of expertise, and sensitivity, our habits of working as a team, our practice and approach of how to "connect people," and our cross-cultural skills constituted decisive elements in the good functioning of both the organization and the work of the delegates.

Dudu Rombauer and Véronique Rioufol, International Youth Parliament
www.caa.org.au/parliament

Alex Bellos in Porto Alegre

The Guardian, January 27, 2001
It's about as far from Davos as you can get, politically, socially and geographically. But the first World Social Forum, which opened this week in Brazil, has the same focus: "The future of economic neo-liberalism." Timed to coincide with its Swiss counterpart, the anti-Davos meeting aims to become an annual fixture to study and propose alternatives to globalization. More than 4,000 delegates from 120 countries are attending the forum, including some high profile intellectuals and activists concerned with the effects of globalization on the world's poor.

The five-day conference aims to provide the global anti-capitalist movement with an intellectual and practical reference point. Its fundamental ideas are well known, and include taxation of speculative capital, the end of tax havens, the complete cancellation of third world debt, and total opposition to liberalizing agricultural markets. Brazil was considered the best host for the meeting because of its variety of social movements and experiments. Porto Alegre, capital of the southernmost Brazilian state of Rio Grande do Sul, was chosen as the location partly because of a sympathetic local government – which contributed about £350,000. In his opening speech, Olivio Dutra, the state governor, said: "The World Social Forum is the opportunity we need to rescue history's most valuable asset: solidarity. It is the tool we need to assure ethics in politics and democracy in social action."

Global Exchange Email Lists

www.globalexchange.org
Global Exchange maintains several email lists related to its campaigns for social and economic justice. Use this site to subscribe to the lists.

Magazines:

Akwe:kon Journal

Akwe:kon Press, 300-T Caldwell Hall, Cornell University, Itchaca, NY 14853, Tel No: (607) 255 4308

Websites:

Global Exchange   www.globalexchange.org

A research, education, and action center building bridges between grassroots movements in the US and Third World.

Fair Trade Foundation   www.fairtrade.org.uk

Oxfam International   www.oxfam.org

Founded in 1995, Oxfam International is an international confederation of 11 autonomous non-government organizations. Member organizations are of diverse cultures, history, and language, but share the commitment to working for an end to the waste and injustice of poverty – both in longer-term development work and in times of urgent humanitarian need. The individual Oxfams work in different ways but have a common purpose: addressing the structural causes of poverty and related injustice. The Oxfams work primarily through local organizations in more than 100 countries.

The Oxfam International Secretariat is a small team of staff that coordinates communication and co-operation between 11 members from its base in Oxford, UK.

The New Internationalist   www.oneworld.org/ni/

World Development Movement   www.wdm.org.uk

Institute for Local Self Reliance (ILSR)   www.ilsr.org

The Institute for Local Self Reliance is a non-profit research and educational organization that provides technical assistance and information on environmentally-sound economic development strategies. Since 1974 ILSR has worked with citizen groups, governments, and private businesses in developing policies that extract the maximum value from local resource.

The Nation *www.thenation.com*

WTO Watch *www.wtowatch.org*

The global information center on the WTO, trade, and sustainable development. Learn more about the issues surrounding the World Trade Organization and find press-related resources and information on the WTO, global trade policy, and sustainable development.

TNI *www.tni.org*

Founded in 1974, TNI is an international network of activist-scholars concerned with analyzing and finding viable solutions to such global problems as militarism and conflict; poverty and marginalization; social injustice; environmental degradation. TNI bridges academia and activism.

DAWN *www.dawn.org.fj*

This is a network of women scholars and activists from the economic South who are working for development alternatives that are equitable, gender-just, and sustainable.

Equal Exchange *www.equalexchange.com*

Worker-owned co-op dedicated to fair trade with small-scale coffee farmers in the developing world.

Focus on the Global South *www.focusweb.org*

Research and advocacy related to international finance and other global issues.

Institute for Agriculture and Trade Policy *www.igc.apc.org/iatp*

Conducts research, education, training, and coalition building in support of environmentally and economically sustainable agriculture and trade policy.

Documentaries

Zapatista – A Big Noise Film can be purchased in the US by calling (877) 773 3773 or via prevailingwinds.org and all profits from the film will be donated to the people of Chiapas in the form of humanitarian aid, promoting much needed food and medical supplies to indigenous communities.

4

ENVIRONMENT

It isn't pollution that's harming the environment.
It's the impuritites in our air and water that are doing it

George W. Bush

MYTH:

Globalization is good for the environment

REALITY:

Economic globalization does not produce wealth, save for a small percentage of people. And the wealth that is produced is rarely spent on environmental programs. The IMF and World Bank practically ensure environmental destruction.

Globalization is inherently destructive to the natural world because it requires that products travel thousands of miles around the planet, resulting in staggering environmental costs such as unprecedented levels of sea and air pollution, increased energy consumption, and use of packaging materials. It also requires devastating new infrastructure developments: new roads, ports, airports, pipelines, and power grids.

WTO agreements have already rolled back years of hard-won environmental gains made through national legislation and multilateral environmental agreements, including measures agreed upon at the 1992 Rio Summit.

In the interests of advancing trade liberalization, commercial interests advising governments say trade rules must be consistent from country to country. Instead of setting minimum standards for environmental protection, WTO agreements and rulings effectively place a ceiling on environmental standards. This ensures that environmental regulations sink to the lowest common denominator.

The wealth that is produced is rarely spent on environmental programs. The IMF and World Bank practically ensure environmental destruction.

Anita: It's frustrating sometimes to see the mismatch in resources between the pointless and the urgent, isn't it. Like the gap between the vast resources poured into military technological research to make war more sophisticated, and the trickle that goes into developing techniques that might prevent war instead. In the same way, there's a gap between the vast sums poured into global financial institutions, from the IMF to the G8 and the new impoverished, powerless environmental institutions. What we need, according to James Morgan, is an E8...

James Morgan Most of us occasionally think about our planet and wonder if we are wrecking it. And most, when thinking a bit more deeply, probably conclude that our grandchildren will inhabit a nastier world than we do. Nastier not because people will be behaving worse, but because global warming could cut food production, because the seas may be empty of fish, and because the range of plant and animal species will be reduced to those few that the 21st century found most useful.

Yet our thoughtful person may still not accept that a blind eye and a shrug of the shoulders are a correct response to the environmental challenge. There is still a feeling that something can be done, beyond giving a little money to Friends of the Earth and cycling to the bottle bank rather than taking the Range Rover.

Governments can do something. But they have to do it in collaboration with other governments or attract the unpopularity of levying petrol taxes that are far higher than those that prevail elsewhere and produce no obviously useful results. Governments disagree among themselves and do not want to make what they like to call "concessions" unless others do more. The United Mineworkers of America become extremely cross when it is suggested that the US should reduce coal emissions. They point out that India has dirtier coal and will soon be burning much more of it. The Indians then ask why they should make sacrifices when the industrial world has already half-wrecked the planet in its ruthless search for prosperity over the last century or so. So why should India be hobbled now?

There is, however, a precedent that shows that something can be done. The Montreal Protocol of 1987, when there was agreement on outlawing CFCs, provides an example of a global bargain. The rather inconclusive agreement on climate-change countermeasures reached at Kyoto in 1997 was at least a step forward. But the search for a responsible fishing policy for the European Union usually results in a couple of steps forward and three back. That last example reflects the contradiction that characterizes attempts to cope with a problem that demands all-round sacrifices: each fishing minister goes in to negotiations determined to obtain a "good" agreement. Which means one that, ideally, damages his country not at all while others stop fishing. Nobody can obtain that: instead there is some ugly horse (or fish) trading and the European fishing industry continues its progress towards self-inflicted extinction.

Fortunately there are some partial solutions. Problems can be alleviated through emissions trading. Agreements on bio-diversity can be made to work through all kinds of schemes, ranging from loans-for-nature to pharmaceutical companies investing in natural biological reserves.

And there could be significant progress if governments could at least come to see problems from a shared perspective. That cannot happen in a world of nearly 200 individual nations, but we don't need as many as that to change the world.

In order to secure meaningful agreements on the kinds of action that might be necessary to save the planet, there are only eight countries that really matter. The Worldwatch Institute in Washington originally came up with the idea of what it calls the Environmental Eight. The E8 consists of three industrial countries – the United States, Japan, and Germany. Then there are two developing countries that seem likely to become industrial giants and major polluters of the future – China and India. Two others contain most of the world's rainforests and much of its biological resources – Brazil and Indonesia. And finally there is, of course, Russia, which defies description.

These countries together hold half the world's population, produce more than half its output, and generate most of its pollutants. They have most of the rainforests and catch most of the fish. They also all have the capacity to do incalculable damage in the future, should they so choose.

Were the E8 to meet once a year, as the G8 does today, we would all have a focus for not only expressing our concerns about where our planet is heading but also for banging heads together. Now, we know that the worst might not happen, but we don't quite know what the worst is. So let us take a look. If greenhouse gases are going to cause the kind of damage most experts forecast, here is a nasty thought. If our planet does warm up by a few degrees, the Siberian permafrost will melt. If the Siberian permafrost melts, more methane will be released from the newly-created million-square-mile swamp than has hit the world in all its history. It is not just the Russians who should be worried.

We face a life of non-linear dynamic change, in other words the world is changing in unpredictable and extraordinarily rapid ways. That is true in our economic and social life. It could also be true in the physical world. In the past, we feared what the planet might do to us, today we fear what we might do to our planet. But we don't have to pretend we can't do anything about it.

James Morgan, former economic researcher and journalist, is the author of *The Last Generation*, a study of the problems of global environmental governance.

Anita: Mess with nature and it will mess right back — that's the law of the GMO jungle.

David Korten The rapid and wide-scale commercialization of transgenic organisms is a new phenomenon. Conventional plant breeding, which involves selective cross breeding between plants of the same or closely related species, simulates natural processes. Genetically engineered plants are by contrast commonly transgenic, meaning they are created by moving genetic material across nature's carefully erected species barriers and inserting them into the cells of a wholly alien species.

Harmful as they are, at least nuclear and chemical wastes do not self-reproduce. Transgenic organisms do. They also mutate and interact with other species – and once released into the environment they may prove impossible to recall or isolate.

Under pressure to rapidly achieve dominant market positions, biotech companies have rushed transgenic organisms to the market with minimal testing or regard for the consequences. By 1999 a hundred million acres were planted in transgenic crops, primarily in the US, Argentina, and Canada. Faced with a growing public outcry from citizen groups alerted to the fact that biotech corporations are playing Russian roulette for profit with the living systems, seven major biotech corporations formed the Council for Biotechnology Information to carry out a $50 million PR campaign to assure the public that their products are both beneficial and harmless.

With billions of dollars at stake, corporations insist that they should be allowed to move ahead with the commercialization of these products until others provide conclusive proof that they are harmful. Yet our understanding of the implications of such technologies for our own bodies and the living systems of the earth remains minuscule. We are like a child with a box of matches sitting next to a container of gasoline armed only with the knowledge that striking a match will produce a pretty flame.

The consequences of leaving it to corporations to make for us such basic decisions about how the genetic environment of the planet will be altered – in some instances permanently and irreversibly – purely on the basis of what is possible and profitable is becoming increasingly foolhardy.

David Korten

By **1999** a **hundred million acres** were **planted** in **transgenic crops, primarily** in the **US, Argentina,** and **Canada.**

Burning off Democracy

When the Canadian government banned the use of a manganese-based additive in gasoline, the US Ethyl Corporation sued under NAFTA. The trade panel ruled that Canada lacked a compelling scientific basis for the law.

Thus Ethyl would be owed considerable compensation for lost potential profits if Canada went ahead. Canada backed down.

David Morris

Three Legs are Better than Two

Anita: In an age as media-saturated as ours, it's vital that you know how to sell your message. Adam Werbach, President of the Sierra Club, once described Randy Hayes as "a radical messenger with the mentality of a Madison Avenue advertising executive who is selling just one thing, saving the world before it is too late." Randy, a dogged activist, founded the Rainforest Action Network (RAN) which has been at the forefront of efforts to halt old growth logging and the fight for the rights of indigenous people. Now with his new group, Destination Conservation, he is leading a major campaign to confront over-consumption and foster energy efficiency. And his "500 Year Plan" reconciles progress and sustainability. All of which means, what Randy is selling, we need to be buying.

Randy Hayes We have all experienced the stability of a three-legged stool. One method of social and ecological change is called the three-legged stool strategy. It applies whether one is trying to halt deforestation, protect rivers, maintain the ocean's fisheries, decrease pesticide use, change business manufacturing processes, or resolve climate change.

- Identify key problems and bring attention to them.
  Find the leverage points for systemic change

- Identify the alternatives to the behavior you don't want.
  Finding profitable alternatives speeds the changes

- Put behavioral change programs in place. In business this
  is called operationalizing new policy

The result is that business as usual stops and new ways of doing business are started.

With groups like Friends of the Earth, Greenpeace, the Ruckus Society, and Rainforest Action, one can see expertise in the first leg and a bit of expertise in the second leg of the stool. Great as these organizations are, it is insufficient in terms of getting the social and ecological changes to happen as quickly as we need. We need help with positive alternatives and handholding to get the behavioral changes.

A few groups have stepped in to help with the process. However, environmental groups that specialize in alternatives and operationalizing change tend to be under-capitalized and are not doing a particularly stellar job. These groups include The Natural Step, World Resources Institute, Global Forest Watch, Certified Wood Products Council, Global Futures, Natural Resource Defense Council, and Forest Trends. I'm not blaming them. Charting new territory is not easy.

I admit some self-interest on behalf of the world's forests, particularly if grants were made to help achieve changes from the growing list of giant home improvement stores and homebuilders.

A foundation executive or board member might ask: Shouldn't companies pay for these services? Yes, they should and some fee for services is already happening. However, business people want value when paying for services. A one time shot

1 Identify key problems and bring attention to them

2 Identify the alternatives to the behavior you don't want

3 Put behavioral change programs in place

of $1 million for three of these groups would allow them to deepen and develop their expertise and the services they offer. These services would also be useful to advocacy groups such as Friends of the Earth, Rainforest Action Network, Greenpeace, Sierra Club, Earth Island, IRN, and Pesticide Action Network.

Research skills in alternative materials and programs to get people to make crucial behavior changes such as conserving energy or mundane tasks such as ordering different office supplies are desperately needed. This will be useful not only to social change organizations and businesses, but for schools, universities, churches, cities, and other government agencies. They all need help fast-tracking changes. With funder support, the groups will have more to offer and be better placed to sustain their work helping society make ecological changes. They could command decent fees for truly useful services.

There is a time to be tough, but tough isn't the goal. Groups like Rainforest Action and Greenpeace will be there when key players like Home Depot are recalcitrant. However, one should always remember how Martin Luther King saw social change. The role of demonstrations is not to win, but to get others to walk with you.

Our social change movement must quickly become better at legs 2 and 3 of the three-legged stool. When we do so, we will speed the transformation. A continued focus in these areas will go a long way toward building a socially just and ecologically sustainable society – if not in our lifetime then at least in our children and grandchildren's lives.

Randy Hayes

Anita: What will it take to turn honorable resolutions into practical solutions?

Michelle Sforza In 1997, representatives from 150 countries convened in Kyoto, Japan to establish legally binding limits on emissions of greenhouse gases. Thirty-seven industrialized nations, including the EU, the US, and Japan, agreed to significantly limit greenhouse gas emissions.

To comply, in 1998 Japan revised its Law Concerning Rational Use of Energy, which includes rules setting standards for automobile fuel efficiency. But when Japan attempted to implement its Kyoto objectives, the US and the EU accused Tokyo of violating WTO rules and began pushing the Japanese to loosen the new emissions standards. Sources within the Japanese government confirmed that the EU and the US objected to the Japanese regulations on behalf of Daimler-Chrysler and Ford. Both companies are members of the Global Climate Coalition, the industry group leading the charge against US Senate ratification of the Kyoto Protocol.

Adapted from an article by
Michelle Sforza in *Multinational Monitor*

View from the Canopy

Anita: Never feel too small or powerless to make a difference.

Julia Butterfly

For 738 days I lived in the canopy of an ancient redwood tree in northern California to protect this magnificent elder, known as Luna, and to help make the world aware of the destruction of our forests.

From my perch 180 feet high I could see barren hillsides, the small timber town where families lost their homes due to a mudslide, and the Pacific Lumber mill where once beautiful forests are converted into lumber. From my treetop perspective it was clear how the industrial logging practices of clearcutting and herbicide destroy wildlife habitat, the quality of our lives, and our communities.

For millennia the two-million acre redwood ecosystem thrived and sheltered myriad species of life. In the last 150 years, 97 percent of the original redwood forests have been destroyed by timber corporations. With only 3 percent of these native forests remaining, species like the marbled murrelet seabird and coho salmon are on the brink of extinction and people fear that they will lose their jobs and futures. Big business cut-and-run logging operations have instilled a false dichotomy: jobs versus the environment. As long as we label each other "loggers and environmentalists" it is difficult to find our common ground and restore the forests and diversity that are our true legacy.

Globalization of natural resources like ancient forests undermines the stability of our watersheds and communites. In order to achieve true sustainability for all life forms we must put our primary needs of fresh air, clean water, and biological and cultural diversity above corporate profit.

We can create a sustainable culture of life on earth by growing and purchasing organic foods, relying on our renewable natural resources like solar and wind power, conserving our precious fresh water, and reducing and revising the "waste" we generate as a society. When we are rooted deeply in love and respect for the interconnectedness of all beings, it becomes a joy to make choices that help sustain life rather than destroy it.

Julia Butterfly

Per Capita **waste production** in **western Europe** has risen **35%** since **1980**

 GEP2000 UNEP

Dying for a Drink! – Water

Anita: Here is one issue with the power to determine the future of us all.

Maude Barlow

Water belongs to the earth and all species. No one has the right to profit from it. By 2025 as much as two-thirds of the world's population will be living in conditions of serious water shortage. Already 31 countries face water scarcity and more than a billion people lack adequate access to drinking water.

Just as we are beginning to face this reality, however, water is being turned into a commodity. Governments all over the world are dismantling environmental legislation or allowing the industry to police itself. Instead of taking care of the limited water we have, we are diverting, polluting, and depleting it at an astonishing rate.

- **Millions of Chinese farmers find their local wells pumped dry**

- **80 percent of China's major rivers are so degraded, they no longer support fish**

- **75 percent of Russia's lake and river water is unsafe to drink**

- **Mexico City is so desperate for water, the entire population may have to be relocated within a decade**

While governments have been slow in coming to terms with this crisis, the private sector has identified water as the last great untapped natural resource to be exploited for profit. Giant transnational water, food, energy, and shipping corporations are doing all in their power to kick-start the trade in "blue gold." Their goal is to make water a private commodity, sold and traded on the open market.

At the heart of environmentalists' many demands is the necessity

• **To use resources frugally**

• **For industry and agriculture to cause minimal pollution**

• **To preserve wildlife, wildernesses, and biodiversity, and**

• **To maximize recycling**

Globalization thwarts this by its mix of trade rules that maximize international competitiveness, with the emphasis on the cheapest product, and the encouragement of inward investment and reduced public expenditure.

**Maude Barlow is national
chairperson of the council of Canadians**

There is **simply no way** to **overstate** the **water crisis** of the **planet today**. Many now **predict** that the **wars of this century** will be **over water**.

 Maude Barlow

Trading away Life

Anita: As far as the WTO is concerned, corporate welfare overrides the public interest.

Multinational monitor

In the WTO's very first ruling on one country's challenge to another's law, a tribunal ordered the US to scrap its Clean Air Act or face economic sanctions because the regulation might adversely impact foreign gasoline. So the Clinton administration moved to change the offending regulation.

Soon afterwards, another WTO tribunal held that a European ban on US beef from hormone-treated cows violated WTO rules requiring countries to prove that products are actually dangerous before taking them off the market (as opposed to requiring companies to demonstrate that products are safe before they are put on the market).

The EU defied the WTO ruling, and is now paying the price: small European family farms are suffering $200 million in retaliatory tariffs against their products each year until the EU revokes the ban.

A quarter of the WTO's enforceable rulings have been against food safety rules, product standards, and environmental regulations. The WTO has never upheld a challenged environmental regulation.

While the WTO has made clear its willingness to override hard-won, domestic public health and environmental laws, it is now becoming increasingly clear that laws adopted to comply with international agreements on the environment are equally vulnerable to challenge under WTO rules.

In 1998, a WTO appellate panel ruled the US could not maintain an embargo on shrimp from countries that have not adopted regulations to protect endangered sea turtles from drowning in shrimp nets. The US took the action under CITES, an agreement signed by over 146 nations to protect animals threatened with extinction.

The WTO panel chose not to interpret the US shrimp embargo as a legitimate exercise of its obligations under CITES, even though the agreement lists the sea turtle as a species that signatory countries must protect.

Source: *Multinational Monitor*

A total of **5.8 million hectares of Latin America** forest was **lost** between **1990 and 1995**

[roughly the size of West Virginia]

Anita: The trouble with the new world we have watched being created over the past decade is that it sees no further than money. People have always been obsessed with money, of course – greed is as old as history. But when the institutions that govern all our lives forget there was ever anything else, then it gets dangerous. When they try to airbrush everything else out of the photographs, like Soviet censors, then we should be really worried. The point about taking it personally is that our ordinary, personal lives are not like that at all. Unlike the new monster institutions and corporations, ordinary people can see very clearly that what is most important in the world does not show up on a balance sheet. When you remember that, and look afresh at an idea like debt, says Andrew Simms, suddenly the world looks very different...

Andrew Simms

People in glass houses shouldn't throw stones. It's the kind of advice that parents love giving to children – heavy with the metaphor, mildly philosophical, and too immediately confusing to argue with.

For years, rich countries and their pocket institutions like the World Bank and IMF have been throwing stones at poor countries, telling them to pay back debts. The debts are often highly dubious – if you dare ask who was to blame for creating them – and are almost always terribly damaging to the lives of the people in the countries that have to pay.

In the age of climate change, it now emerges that the stone-throwers are living in a glass house of their own making. By recklessly burning more than their fair share of fossil fuels, rich countries have run up a huge environmental debt, a carbon debt, and it's time to call them to account. The world they are creating is an increasingly fragile and hostile place.

On 1 March 2000, the world's media reported a story of hope amid the despair and catastrophe of Mozambique's massive floods. For days, while the international response stalled, just a handful of helicopters plucked a lucky few stranded people to safety. Then a woman was found clinging to a tree to escape the floodwater. She had been there for three days. Extraordinarily, in the minutes before her rescue, she gave birth. There was a ripple of inappropriate self-congratulation in the Western press.

The story diverted attention from the large but unknown number of deaths, the estimated one million people displaced, the loss of countless livestock and crops, the immeasurable damage to infrastructure. Typically, poverty had moved large numbers of people into areas that were highly vulnerable to climate-related disasters.

For a country still recovering from years of conflict and debt, the flood not only wiped out hard-won human development gains, but blighted the country far into the foreseeable future. In spite of its poverty and efforts towards reform, the servicing of foreign debts had been allowed to drain Mozambique of precious resources for many years.

Even after the latest debt-relief deal, estimates suggested that Mozambique would still have to spend $45 million a year on debt servicing – more than it spent on either primary health care or basic education.

Yet, while highly indebted poor countries are pursued by creditors to service their foreign debts, industrialized countries are themselves responsible for a larger and potentially more damaging ecological debt. No accounting system exists yet to force repayment of carbon debt – and so far, those most responsible are least likely to suffer the consequences. But the specter of global warming darkens everyone's horizon. According to a letter signed in December 1999 by the under-secretary of the US National Oceanic and Atmospheric Administration and the chief executive of the UK Meteorological Office, "the rapid rate of warming since 1976, approximately 0.20 Celsius per decade, is consistent with the projected rate of warming based on human-induced effects. We continue to see confirmation of the long-term warming trend." Also, a consensus is growing that climate change could soon spiral out of control when it passes a critical threshold thanks to the process of "positive feedback."

Poor people in poor countries suffer first and worst from extreme weather conditions linked to climate change. Today, 96 percent of all deaths from natural disasters occur in developing countries. By 2025, over half of all people living in developing countries will be "highly vulnerable" to floods and storms. Ironically, these are also the people likely to be most affected by the results of financial debt.

Mozambique is just one example. Late in 1999, the coasts of Venezuela and India's Orissa state suffered some of the worst storms and flooding in living memory, killing tens of thousands. Ever-worsening floods in Bangladesh left 21 million homeless in 1998. That same year, the El Niño weather phenomenon left its scar of droughts and floods from southern Africa to northern India, Latin America to the Pacific. Then, ironically, Mozambique had to prepare for drought. When Hurricane Mitch hit Central America, the Honduran president pointed out: "We lost in 72 hours what we have taken more than 50 years to build." According to the reinsurance giant MunichRe, the number of weather-related and flood disasters quadrupled during the 1990s compared to the 1960s, while resulting economic losses increased eight-fold over the same period.

To solve the problem or, at least, mitigate its worst effects, all nations will have to live within one global environmental budget. Emissions need controlling because the atmosphere, seas, and forests can only absorb a certain amount before disruption begins. Currently, industrialized countries generate more than 62 times more carbon dioxide pollution per person than the least developed countries. An average US citizen pollutes at about 12 times the sustainable global rate per person.

No one owns the atmosphere, yet we all depend upon it. So we can assume that we all have an equal right to its services – an equal right to pollute. On the basis of the minimum cuts in total carbon dioxide pollution needed to stabilize the climate – estimated by the Intergovernmental Panel on Climate Change to be between 60 and 80 percent of the pollution levels reached in 1990 – rich countries are running up a massive carbon debt. By using fossil fuels at a level far above a threshold for sustainable consumption, year after year the carbon debts of rich countries get bigger.

The challenge is now to devise sustainability adjustment programs for the rich. Klaus Töpfer, executive director of the UNEP, has called for a 90 percent cut in consumption in rich countries to meet the challenge. Töpfer, in UNEP's, "Global Environmental Outlook 2000," pointed to global warming as one of the main threats to the human race, and added that "a series of looming crises and ultimate catastrophe can only be averted by a massive increase in political will."

Any solution to climate change will need to be based on reductions in emissions. We will also have to move towards equally sharing the atmosphere. To manage a period of transition people will need to be able to trade the right to pollute. But you cannot trade what you do not own. That means not a redistribution of our ownership rights, but a pre-distribution of our equal entitlements to the atmosphere.

After decades of a system that has driven the gap between rich and poor ever wider, we arrive at a devastating conclusion. Climate change has created a new debt, the opposite of the familiar deadweight that hangs around the necks of poor countries and now, as if to mock the endless squabbling of political ideologues we realize, sitting in our glasshouse, that now our very survival depends on equity.

Andrew Simms is the head of the Global Economy Program of the New Economics Foundation.

Anita: We never planned on good genes going the way of the dodo.

David Korten In 1996, when Theo Colborn and her research team published "Our Stolen Future" the public first became aware of the full implications of the 70,000 synthetic chemicals now dispersed in the environment.

Thousands of these chemicals mimic the action of hormones in humans and other living creatures and are responsible for declining sperm counts; reproductive failures; a high incidence of deformities in frogs, fish, and birds; and the impaired intellectual and behavioral development of human children.

David Korten

Climate Change and Globalization

Anita: Greenpeace embodies the mantra "think globally, act locally." It can mobilize the support of well over 2.5 million supporters in 140 countries to focus on environmental issues in a way that is most meaningful to each locality. Since the early 1970s, those issues have included climate protection, nuclear testing, and GMO's. And the success of every single campaign has boiled down to as many people as possible taking it personally – taking personal action, however small or grand that may be. Greenpeace is committed to creating solutions – offering choices – that fit easily into everyday life. In the case of climate change, it's the choice between buying dirty, dangerous, and outdated fossil fuels, or buying clean, safe, hi-tech, and inexhaustible renewable ("green") energy. But in order for the supply of "green" energy to open up, YOU must demand it. Then demand will be met with supply, and the market place will shift from negative to positive energy.

"It is necessary to destroy the village in order to save it from communism" was the kind of thing the US military used to say in the Vietnam war back in the '60s. Today, the world's addiction to fossil fuels – that's coal, oil, and gas to you and me – has the same crazy twisted logic, threatening to wreck the environment on which we all depend. In just a few decades, our addiction to these fuels has driven up levels of heat-trapping gases in the Earth's atmosphere to levels not seen in millions of years.

The overwhelming majority of the world's top climate scientists paint a horrendous picture of the greenhouse world we risk creating unless we cut down on the emission of gases like carbon dioxide. In Europe we will experience more storms and floods. Glaciers and polar ice caps will continue melting, so that we may lose the Greenland and Antarctic ice sheets completely. This could add around 6 metres to global sea level, with catastrophic effects.

But the greatest impacts will be on the world's poorest people in parts of Africa and Asia — those least able to protect themselves from rising sea levels and increased drought and disease. Tens of millions of people will lose their homes as a result of flooding and tropical cyclones. Responsibility lies overwhelmingly with the richest countries: Europe, North America, Japan, and Australia. With just 20 percent of the world's population we have the longest track record of climate pollution and are still by far the biggest climate wreckers. Our behavior is nothing but arrogant in the extreme — some go as far as to call it "carbon aggression." And what do we use it for? In an increasingly globalized economy, we waste it on massive movements of energy-intensive goods and services over longer and longer distances. Even the materials that go to make a simple drink can have traveled thousands of miles.

Then we throw the can away, and the whole process is repeated. Economic growth is good news when it delivers real improvements in quality of life — such as better education and healthcare, more nutritious food, more time for family and community. But growth which undermines the very fabric of nature on which we depend is mad.

Growth for its own sake is the ideology of a cancer cell. We have to move away from a dumb economy that chews up, spits out and destroys nature and people towards a smart one which operates within natural cycles: we need to learn to live within limits. This doesn't mean poverty. It means a different kind of wealth. It means endless opportunities for appropriate and environmental technologies, for locally-produced food.

The world desperately needs this kind of "smart growth." It means more than just PR. A company like BP spends millions re-branding itself as a company that is moving "beyond petroleum." But the amount it spends on advertising this "new" image is far more than it actually spends on renewable energy sources such as solar power and the development of a hydrogen-based economy, which could run all our homes, cars, and industry without any pollution at all. There are mechanisms within the international climate treaty signed at Kyoto, and rejected by US President Bush, to help the transfer of clean technology to the developing world so that these nations can improve their standard of living and grow their economies without traveling along the same polluting road as the industrialized world.

Sorting out the current mess isn't going to be plain sailing. But we know where to start. We'll need international solidarity and strong international environmental and social agreements which help people to do more of what they need at a local level. Above all, we'll need more democracy. Some call it "Glocal-ization."

Doing as much as we can locally doesn't mean an end to free trade. It means an end to rigged trade, which exploits the poor and trashes the environment by not paying the full environmental and social costs.

The billions being spent on new oil exploration should be spent on getting out of dangerous and dirty fossil fuels, and getting into clean and safe renewable technologies, like solar photovoltaic panels (PV) for instance, which could provide electricity for the two billion people in the world who don't have access to it while creating new jobs and helping to make communities more self-reliant and stronger.

This is one of the biggest business opportunities of all time. So the denial of global warming is economically stupid, as well as scientifically illiterate and morally bankrupt.

Greenpeace

Rainforest Action Network

www.ran.org

The lungs of the planet, the pharmacy of the future – the rainforests of the world get lumbered with a lot of responsibility. But the plain fact is, these ancient ecosystems are essential for all life on earth. Among the vital functions they perform: stabilizing the Earth's climate, preserving wildlife habitat, and maintaining soil productivity.

And yet, for all their value, the rainforests are an appallingly abused asset, badly in need of some radical help. It was with this in mind that Randy Hayes founded the Rainforest Action Network in 1985, with the stated mission to protect the Earth's rainforests and support the rights of their inhabitants through education, grassroots organizing, and non-violent direct action.

Since its launch, RAN has been a world leader in rainforest conservation. It has educated and mobilized consumers and community action groups throughout the United States, through means as diverse as student information packages, grassroots skills training, and websites. And RAN works alongside environmental and human rights groups in dozens more countries, offering financial support and networking services to indigenous and environmental activists seeking ecologically sustainable solutions within their own regions.

The strengths of RAN's grassroots activism were obvious from its first direct-action campaign in 1987. It organized a boycott of Burger King, which was importing cheap beef from tropical countries where rainforests were being stripped to provide pasture for cattle. When sales dropped 12 per cent during the boycott, Burger King cancelled $35 million worth of beef contracts in Central America and announced it would no longer buy beef from the rainforest.

The success of the Burger King boycott taught American citizens that, if their consumption patterns could contribute to problems in far-off rainforests, they could equally contribute to solutions, not just through their purchasing power but also through letter-writing and public non-violent demonstrations, turning concern into effective action.

Another success has been RAN's Old Growth Campaign, which works to preserve the Earth's remaining ancient forests by driving old growth wood products out of the marketplace and by promoting the use of sustainable alternatives. In 1999, in response to an international campaign led by RAN, Home Depot "the single largest retailer of lumber in the world" agreed to phase out its sales of old growth wood. Most of the home construction industry has followed suit and other industry leaders such as Kinkos, 3M, IBM, Hallmark, and Hewlett-Packard have adopted strict policies prohibiting the purchase of old growth pulp, paper, and lumber.

RAN is also currently running Campaign for a Sane Economy, which pinpoints the roots of environmental devastation in the global financial system which encourages corporations to seek short-term profit at any cost. The particular target of this campaign is Citigroup, the largest financial institution in America and a key player in financing many of the world's most environmentally destructive development projects. RAN is, in its own words, challenging a definition of profit that fails to recognize the value of protecting the environment, preserving democracy, and building a just and equitable global society.

Boycott

E$$O

No.1 global warming villain

www.stopesso.com

The UN Intergovernmental Panel on Climate Change (IPCC), made up of the world's top scientists, has recently confirmed that the world is warming up at a rate much faster than originally predicted. By 2080, 94 million people around the world will be at risk from flooding every year as a result of global warming; 290 million more will be at risk from malaria. By 2025, two out of three people could lack sufficient water, and drought will cause widespread famine.

And for all of this, we can blame our runaway use of fossil fuels such as oil.

And we can blame and shame corporations like Esso. Esso (known as ExxonMobil in the USA) produces four million barrels of oil a day. Last year, their profits were $17.7 billion (£12 billion), more than any other company has ever made. That makes them the biggest polluters on the face of the planet. And here's what they are doing with their money:

- Esso is currently spending £5.5 billion on oil and gas exploration and production and not one penny on clean renewable energy sources like wind, wave or solar power. Their competitors BP and Shell are at least beginning to see the light and investigating renewable energy alternatives. Meanwhile, Esso lobbies for access to the pristine Arctic National Wildlife Refuge.

- Esso campaigns vigorously against the Kyoto Protocol, the international agreement to cut greenhouse gas emissions, and any other international action on climate change. Esso deny claims of a link between their business and global warming, but doubts have been voiced concerning the reliability of evidence supporting this claim. The author of a report on temperature change in the Sargasso Sea stated "I think the sad thing is ExxonMobil is exploiting the data for political purposes."

- Esso invested $1,086,080 – more than any other oil company – in George W. Bush's election campaign. As soon as he became president, he said the

United States would pull out of Kyoto and other international agreements to stop global warming – exactly the policy Esso was promoting.

But if Esso chooses to wreck our climate, we can choose not to buy Esso's products. Here's all you need to do to take action:

1.Sign the on-line pledge at www.stopesso.com

2.Don't use Esso petrol stations until their parent company, ExxonMobile, starts supporting the Kyoto protocol, instead of trying to kill it.

The worst nightmare of companies like Esso's is a customer revolt. Help make their nightmare come true.

Take it Personally

Become a green consumer.
Think before you buy.

Most green action groups have useful websites where you can join specific campaigns to put pressure on politicians and offending companies. Check them out. Become a green consumer. Think before you buy. Avoid "dirty" companies' products if possible. Try to find second uses for items you might normally throw away. Use as little electricity, water, and gas as you can. Think green and spread the word.

Greenpeace Activists recently sealed off a genetic engineering research center on Canada's Prince Edward Island. A/F Protein has applied to the US Food and Drug Administration for permission to commercialize genetically modified salmon.

GE fish have the potential to cause irreversible damage to wild fish stocks and to the wider marine environment. Leading marine biologists have expressed grave reservations and warned that even a small number of GE fish released into the wild can have potentially devastating effects. Researchers at Purdue University in Indiana estimate that 60 fertile GE fish introduced into a natural population of 60,000 could annihilate the natural stock in 20–30 years. A/F Protein's application to commercialize GE salmon for the aquaculture industry worldwide is currently being considered by the United States Food and Drug Administration (FDA) under their regulation on "animal drugs," and a ruling is expected anytime this year. The permit would set a precedent for approvals of other types of GE fish that are already being developed, including trout, catfish, lobster, carp, and striped bass. The company A/F Protein claims that it already has orders for 15 million GE fish eggs for delivery as soon as the FDA gives the go-ahead.

Tens of thousands of angry citizens from all over the world "flooded" the White House with e-mails, as a part of a Friends of the Earth protest over Bush's climbdown on the UN climate treaty, the Kyoto Protocol. The White House server reportedly crashed twice, unable to process the world-wide protest. At peak times, every second an e-protest was sent.

More than 50,000 people from all continents participated, including representatives from industry, governments, churches, parliaments and NGOs. Some 200 people from the European Commission were among the protesters as well as employees of BP and Shell, using their office computers. Messages came from every corner of the world, from Patagonia to Portugal, from Tasmania to Texas, from China to Costa Rica. The protest has been translated into French, German, Spanish, Russian, Japanese. More than 2,000 US citizens even sent a fax to the White House.

The form e-mail read:

Dear President Bush,

I call on you as President of the USA not to betray the Kyoto Protocol.

The United States must live up to its commitment to the UN negotiations to prevent global warming. Sabotaging the Kyoto Protocol puts the USA into a position of environmental isolationism and makes it responsible for climate catastrophe. The US has one of the highest per capita CO_2 emissions in the world. People around the world already faced with the first signs of climate change, suffering from floods and hurricanes, expect your country to be in the forefront of tackling climate change.

An enormous potential of creativity, innovation and efficiency is there to be harvested once we have decided to really reduce CO_2 emissions. If you fail to reverse your decision to kill the Kyoto Protocol, future generations will not forgive you.

President Bush, the science is clear and the international political will is there to tackle climate change. The US must join the world in fighting global warming!
Sincerely,
xxxxxxxxx

And the response from the White House was:

Thank you for emailing President Bush. Your ideas and comments are very important to him.

Unfortunately, because of the large volume of email received, the President cannot personally respond to each message...

Sincerely,
The White House Office of E-Correspondence

www.greenpeace.org

The Ecologist *www.theecologist.org*

Founded in 1970, *The Ecologist* is the world's oldest environmental magazine. Its breadth is wide: to rethink the basic assumption behind today's environmental, economic, political, and social problems. With ecological thinkers, political and social commentators, and renowned scientists among the contributors, *The Ecologist* is essential reading.

Resurgence *www.resurgence.org*

Resurgence publishes articles that are on the cutting edge of current thinking, promoting creativity, ecology, spirituality, and frugality. It also runs a great website.

Mother Jones *www.motherjones.com*

Prevailing Winds Research Catalogue *www.prevailingwinds.org*

Reprints, articles etc. Topics include Media Manipulation, War & Terrorism, Financial Scandals, Covert Operations and Drug Cartels, The Hemp Conspiracy. Also sells audio cassettes, video presentations, CD-Rom, and books.

E Magazine *www.emagazine.com*

Rainforest Action Network *www.ran.org*

Since it was founded in 1985, the Rainforest Action Network has been working to protect tropical rainforests and the human rights of those living in and around those forests, strengthening the rainforest conservation movement, supporting activists, and mobilizing consumers and community action groups in the US.

Greenpeace USA *www.greenpeace.org*

Greepeace is an independent campaigning organization that uses non-violent, creative confrontation to expose global environmental problems, and to force solutions that are essential to a green and peaceful future.

Friends of the Earth *www.foe.org*
International environmental group.

EF Schumacher Society *www.schumachersociety.org*
The EF Schumacher Society is an organization that is implementing and spreading the vision of ecologically-based economics. It is developing models for local economic institutions, it has an extensive library on ecological economies, and serves as a clearinghouse for local currency projects.

Sierra Club *www.sierraclub.org*
Founded in 1892, the Sierra club is the leading US grassroots conservation organization. Its goal is the exploration, enjoyment, and protection of the wild places of the Earth.

The Worldwatch Institute *www.worldwatch.org*
The institute is dedicated to fostering the evolution of an environmentally-sustainable society – where human needs do not threaten the health of the natural environment or the prospects of future generations.

Council for Responsible Genetics *www.gene-watch.org*
The Council for Responsible Genetics is a 30-year-old organization of scientists and activists who encourage public participation in debating the social and ethical implications of biotechnology. The Council publishes *Gene Watch* magazine, conducts studies and runs a "No Patents on Life" campaign.

Best environmental directories *www.ulb.ac.be/ceese/meta/cds.html*

Freeplay *www.freeplay.net*
The pioneer and world leader of self powered energy: the concept, the technology, the products, and the industry which empower the user to put human energy into a range of electronic products, and make them work.

World Wildlife Fund *www.wwf.org*

International Institute for Environment & Development *www.iied.org*

MONEY

5

He who knows that enough is enough
will always have enough
Lao-Tzu

MYTH

Economic globalization is inevitable

REALITY:

Advocates of economic globalization try to describe it as an inevitable process, the logical outcome of economic and technological forces that evolved over centuries to their present form, as if they were forces of nature.

But economic globalization is not some accident of evolution. The primary function of bodies like the World Bank, the IMF, GATT, NAFTA, and the WTO is to place economic values above all others, and to establish rules that suppress the ability of nation-states to protect nature, workers, consumers, and even national sovereignty and democracy if they appear to hamper "free" trade. But none of it is inevitable.

To call what is essentially a collection of rules "inevitable," is designed to make everyone feel nothing can be done about it, thus promoting passivity.

How a collective insanity has taken a grip on the world

Anita: The predominant idea behind globalization, in its most virulent form, is an unpleasant kind of social Darwinism – that the world is for winners not losers, that only the successful count, that money is considerably more important than votes. Half a century on since the defeat of Hitler, if that philosophy isn't a distant cousin of fascism then I don't know what is. One brave academic who has done more than almost anyone else to expose the short-comings of this big idea is Susan George. This is her brilliant explanation of how a collective insanity has taken a grip on the world.

Susan George Some 50 years ago if you had seriously proposed any of the ideas and policies in today's standard neo-liberal toolkit, you would have been laughed off the stage or sent off to the insane asylum. At least in the Western countries at that time, everyone was a Keynesian, a social democrat or a social-Christian democrat, or some shade of Marxist. The idea that the market should be allowed to make major social and political decisions; the idea that the state should voluntarily reduce its role in the economy, or that corporations should be given total freedom, that trade unions should be curbed and citizens given less, rather than more, social protection – such ideas were utterly foreign to the spirit of the time.

However incredible it may sound today, the IMF and the World Bank were seen as progressive institutions. When they were created at Bretton Woods in 1944, their mandate was to help prevent future conflicts by lending for reconstruction and development and by smoothing out temporary balance of payments problems. They had no control over individual government's economic decisions nor did their mandate include a license to intervene in national policy.

In the Western nations, the Welfare State and the New Deal had got under way in the 1930s but their spread had been interrupted by the World War II. The first order of business in the post-war world was to put them back in place. The other major item on the agenda was to get world trade moving – and this was accomplished through the Marshall Plan, which established Europe once again as the major trading partner for the USA.

What is Neo-Liberalism?

"Neo-liberalism" is a set of economic policies. You can see its effects as the rich grow richer and the poor grow poorer.

Neo-liberalism in a nutshell:

THE RULE OF THE MARKET

Liberating "free" enterprise from any bonds imposed by the government no matter how much social damage this causes.

CUTTING PUBLIC EXPENDITURE FOR SOCIAL SERVICES

like education and health care and water supply, all in the name of reducing government's role.

DEREGULATION

of laws that could reduce profits, including measures to protect workers and the environment.

PRIVATIZATION

Selling state-owned enterprises, goods, and services to private investors. Although done in the name of greater efficiency, which is often needed, privatization concentrates wealth into fewer hands and makes the public pay more.

ELIMINATING THE CONCEPT OF "THE PUBLIC GOOD"

and replacing it with "individual responsibility." Pressuring the poorest people to find solutions to their lack of health care, education, and social security and branding them, if they fail, as "lazy."

Thanks to Elizabeth Martinez and Arnoldo Garcia.

On the whole, the world had signed on for an extremely progressive agenda. The great scholar Karl Polanyi published his masterwork, *The Great Transformation*, in

1944, a fierce critique of 19th century industrial, market-based society. Over 50 years ago, Polanyi made this amazingly prophetic and modern statement: "To allow the market mechanism to be sole director of the fate of human beings and their natural environment... would result in the demolition of society." But Polanyi was convinced that such a demolition could no longer happen in the post-war world. Alas, his optimism was misplaced: the whole point of neo-liberalism is that the market mechanism should be allowed to direct the fate of human beings. The economy should dictate its rules to society, not the other way around.

So what happened? How did neo-liberalism ever emerge from its ghetto to become the dominant doctrine in the world today?

- **Why can the IMF and the World Bank intervene at will and force countries to participate in the world economy on unfavorable terms?**

- **Why is the Welfare State under threat in all the countries where it was established?**

- **Why is the environment on the edge of collapse?**

- **Why are there so many poor people in both the rich and the poor countries at a time when there has never existed such great wealth?**

One explanation for this triumph of neo-liberalism – and the economic, political, social, and ecological disasters that go with it – is that neo-liberals have bought and paid for their own vicious and regressive "Great Transformation." They have understood, as progressives have not, that ideas have consequences. Starting from a tiny embryo at the University of Chicago with the philosopher-economist Friedrich von Hayek and his students like Milton Friedman, the neo-liberals and their funders have created a huge international network of foundations, institutes, research centers, publications, scholars, writers, and public relations hacks to develop, package, and push their ideas and doctrine relentlessly.

They have built this highly efficient ideological cadre because they understand that if you can occupy people's heads, their hearts and their hands will follow. The ideological and promotional work of the Right has been absolutely brilliant. They have spent hundreds of millions of dollars, but the result has been worth every penny to them because they have made neo-liberalism seem as if it were the natural and normal condition of humankind.

No matter how many disasters the neo-liberal system has created, no matter what financial crises it may engender, no matter how many losers and outcasts it may create, it is still made to seem inevitable, like an act of God, the only possible economic and social order available to us. Let me stress how important it is to understand that this vast neo-liberal experiment we are all being forced to live under has been created by people with a purpose. Once you grasp this, once you understand that neo-liberalism is not a force like gravity but a totally artificial construct, you can also understand that what some people have created, other people can change.

So, from a small, unpopular sect with virtually no influence, neo-liberalism has become the major world religion with its dogmatic doctrine, its priesthood, its law-giving institutions and, perhaps most important of all, its hell for heathens and sinners who dare to contest the Revealed Truth.

The central value of of neo-liberalism is the notion of competition, because it separates the sheep from the goats, the men from the boys, the fit from the unfit. It is supposed to allocate all resources, whether physical, natural, human, or financial with the greatest possible efficiency. In contrast, the great Chinese philosopher Lao Tzu ended his Tao-te Ching with these words: "Above all, do not compete."

The only actors in the neo-liberal world who seem to have taken this advice are the largest actors of all, the transnational corporations. The principle of competition scarcely applies to them: they prefer to practice what we could call Alliance Capitalism. It is no accident that, depending on the year, two-thirds to three-quarters of all the money labeled "foreign direct investment" is not devoted to new, job-creating investment but to mergers and acquisitions which almost invariably result in job losses. But because competition is always a virtue, its results cannot be bad. For the neo-liberal, the market is so wise and so good that like God, the Invisible Hand can bring good out of apparent evil. People are unequal by nature, but this is good because the contributions of the well-born, the best-educated, the toughest, will eventually benefit everyone. Nothing in particular is owed to the weak, the poorly educated: what happens to them is their own fault, never the fault of society. If the competitive system is "given vent" as Mrs Thatcher used to say, society will be the better for it. Unfortunately, the history of the past 20 years teaches us that exactly the opposite is the case.

Another implication of competition as the central value of neo-liberalism is that the public sector must be brutally downsized because it does not and cannot obey the basic law of competing for profits or for market share. Privatization is one of the major economic transformations of the past 20 years. The trend began in Britain and has spread throughout the world.

So why did capitalist countries, particularly in Europe, have public services to begin with? Nearly all public services constitute what economists call "natural monopolies." A company has to be a certain size to realize economies of scale and thus provide the best possible service at the lowest possible cost to the consumer. Public services also require very large investment outlays at the beginning – like railroad tracks or power grids – which does not encourage competition. That's why public monopolies were the obvious optimum solution. But neo-liberals define anything public as "inefficient."

So what happens when a natural monopoly is privatized? Quite normally and naturally, the new capitalist owners tend to impose monopoly prices on the public, while richly remunerating themselves. Classical economists call this outcome "structural market failure" because prices are higher than they ought to be and service to the consumer is not necessarily good. In order to prevent structural market failures, up to the mid-1980s, the capitalist countries of Europe almost universally entrusted the post office, telecoms, electricity, gas, railways, public transport, and other services like water and rubbish collection to state-owned monopolies.

Exactly the same mechanisms have been at work throughout the world. In Britain, the Adam Smith Institute was the intellectual partner for creating the privatization ideology. USAID and the World Bank have also used Adam Smith experts and have pushed the privatization doctrine in the South. By 1991, the Bank had already made 114 loans to speed the process, and every year its Global Development Finance report lists hundreds of privatizations carried out in the Bank's borrowing countries. I submit that we should stop talking about privatization and use words that tell the truth: we are talking about alienation and surrender of the product of decades of work by thousands of people to a tiny minority of large investors. This is one of the greatest hold-ups of ours or any generation.

Lest you thought I had forgotten Ronald Reagan, let me illustrate this point with the observations of Kevin Phillips, a Republican analyst who charted the way Reagan's neo-liberal doctrine and policies had changed American income distribution between 1977 and 1988. These policies were largely elaborated by the conservative Heritage Foundation, the principal think-tank of the Reagan administration and still an important force in American politics. Over the decade of the 1980s, the top 10 percent of American families increased their average family income by 16 percent, the top 5 percent increased theirs by 23 percent, but the extremely lucky top one percent of American families could thank Reagan for a 50 percent increase. As for poorer Americans, the bottom 80 percent all lost something; true to the rule, the lower they were on the scale, the more they lost. The bottom 10 percent of Americans reached the nadir: according to Phillip's figures, they lost 15 percent of their already meager incomes.

There is nothing mysterious about this trend towards greater inequality. Policies are specifically designed to give the already rich more disposable income, particularly through tax cuts and by pushing down wages. The theory and ideological justification for such measures is that higher incomes for the rich and higher profits will lead to more investment, better allocation of resources and therefore more jobs and welfare for everyone. In reality, moving money up the economic ladder has led to stock market bubbles, untold paper wealth for the few, and financial crises. If income is redistributed towards the bottom 80 percent of society, it will be used for consumption and consequently benefit employment. If wealth is redistributed towards the top, where people already have most of the things they need, it will go not into the local or national economy, but to international stock markets.

The same policies have been carried out throughout the South and East under the guise of structural adjustment, which is merely another name for neo-liberalism.

At the international level, neo-liberals have concentrated all their efforts on three fundamental points:

- **Free trade in goods and services**

- **Free circulation of capital**

- **Freedom of investment**

Over the past 20 years, the IMF has been strengthened enormously. Thanks to the debt crisis and the mechanism of conditionality, it has moved from balance of payments support to being the quasi-universal dictator of so-called "sound" economic policies, meaning of course neo-liberal ones. The WTO was finally put in place in January 1995 after long and laborious negotiations, often rammed through parliaments which had little idea what they were ratifying.

The common denominator of these institutions is their lack of transparency and democratic accountability. This is the essence of neo-liberalism. It claims that the economy should dictate its rules to society, not the other way around. Democracy is an encumbrance: neo-liberalism is designed for winners, not for voters who necessarily encompass the categories of both winners and losers.

I submit that neo-liberalism has changed the fundamental nature of politics. Politics used to be primarily about who ruled whom and who got what share of the pie. Aspects of both these central questions remain, of course, but the great new central question of politics is, in my view: "Who has a right to live and who does not." Radical exclusion is now the order of the day.

Susan George is associate director of the Transnational Institute in Amsterdam and president of the Observatoire de la Mondialisation [Globalization Observatory] in Paris.

Ralph Nader:
The Professional Citizen

Anita: Ralph Nader calls himself "a professional citizen." His faith in the citizen as the main agent of change at the heart and soul of the political process has been an inspiration to millions. After all, his own successes have been a sterling endorsement of just how much difference one driven individual can make. All his life, Nader has played David to the corporate Goliath, exposing the iniquities, the greed, and the shortsightedness of the multinationals and standing up for common sense and human decency. Perhaps that's why he shows up in opinion polls as one of the few people in Washington that ordinary Americans trust.

Anita Roddick

Ralph Nader's offer to Congress was a typical gesture from a man who stands for unimpeachable principle in American politics, a public arena that is anything but principled.

The defining themes of Nader's 37-year career as a consumer advocate have been democracy, accountability, and empowerment. It was his sense of the possibilities and obligations of citizenship that drove him to take on General Motors in 1965 – and to run for president in 2000. Among the landmark pieces of legislation he's been responsible for since then are the Motor Vehicle Highway Safety Acts, the Clean Water Act, the Clean Air Act, and the Freedom of Information Act. No target has been too big for "Nader's Raiders," the activists who've been drawn to him over the years. Today, more than 150,000 people are involved in the six branches of Public Citizen, the organization Nader formed in 1971 to work for consumer justice and government and corporate accountability.

Nader has always been acutely sensitive to the relationship between multinational corporations and governments, which intensifies with the passage of autocratic trade treaties like the North American Free Trade Agreement (NAFTA) and the new General Agreement on Tariffs and Trade (GATT). As long ago as 1970, Nader foreshadowed the inevitability of an alliance between consumer and environmental activism when he wrote, "The modern corporation's structure, impact, and public accountability are the central issues in any program designed to curb or forestall the contamination of air, water, and soil by industrial activity."

Because the consumer movement deals with real issues that have an immediate impact on people's lives, it can build campaigns in a way that many other movements can not. It has the power to frighten corporations and governments because it asks questions that must be answered. And, unlike government or law, it can be as global as business itself is. Food or water safety, for instance, is an issue that transcends all national boundaries. Using the inspirational example of Nader's Raiders, dozens of countries now have their own flourishing consumer movements. So Nader's reach keeps pace with his corporate targets.

His call to citizen action will be his most enduring legacy because, as Nader himself explains, "Citizen action in one area connects up with others, a phenomenon I call the 'seamless web of justice.' My theory is that even if you start in a tiny, little area of civic justice, you'll always find it connected to another area, and another – and it gets broader and broader. And we suddenly realize that it's not only in the environment that everything's connected to everything else, but also in the area of justice."

Anita Roddick

Do our leaders read?

"The Final Act Embodying the Results of the Uruguay Round of Multilateral Trade Negotiations" was enacted in 1994, in Marrakech.

It paved the way for the new WTO and gave that body the ability to overrule or undermine international conventions, acts, treaties, and agreements.

When the 550-page agreement was sent to Congress for ratification, Ralph Nader offered to donate $10,000 to the charity of a congressman's choice if any of them signed an affidavit saying they had read it, and could answer several questions about it.

Only one – Senator Hank Brown, a Colorado Republican – took up the challenge. But after reading the document, Brown changed his mind and voted against the agreement.

Your Money or Your Life

Anita: The trouble for those of us in the business world who are trying to make a difference is that the rules are increasingly stacked against us. All too often, the most innovative businesses, genuinely trying to make a difference, are undermined by those that are not. And in the same way, the most committed people – dedicated to making the effects of globalization more personal for all of us – are undermined by the least committed. Or they are ridiculed by the financial media – all too often an echo chamber for the status quo – or they are targeted by the regulators. David Korten's work has made an enormous contribution towards exposing the subtle corruption at the heart of the system...

David Korten Everything seemed to be on the auction block – from water, air, information, indigenous knowledge, seeds and genetic codes, to health care, schools, and prisons – turning public services into private services for those who could afford to pay. It was as if civilization and the planet's life support system had become identified as threats to human well being and the whole of humanity's economic, intellectual, and political resources were being focused on the task of systematically eliminating them.

Since those early meetings there has been an acceleration in the process of depleting the living capital of society and planet for the sole purpose of making money for those who already have far more than they need. This is the reality behind the protests. In April 2000, Business Week observed that there is no longer any pretense of objectivity in television reporting on the financial markets. "Most analysts no longer act as information providers, but as stock promoters." Commentators pushed stocks and hyped the bubble – buy recommendations outnumbered sell recommendations by 72 to 1. Value investing – buying stocks for the long term on the basis of the underlying value of the company – was out. Momentum investing – quickly buying and thenselling a stock exhibiting short-term upward momentum – was in. A decade earlier investors held a NASDAQ stock on average for 2 years. By 2000 the average was 5 months.

SHELL

Corporations have also stepped up their spending on glossy advertising campaigns professing their deep social and environmental commitment. Shell's advertisement in the October 1999 National Geographic featuring pictures of pristine rainforests and touting Shell's commitment to working with indigenous peoples is an especially cynical example.

Shell should know that glossy ads will not erase the memory of the Ogoni leaders hanged by the Nigerian government for protesting against Shell's devastation of their homelands. One can only wonder at how different the world might be if the money spent on such corporate greenwash was devoted instead to cleaning up production operations and improving the lives of people in the impacted areas.

The banking system creates money out of nothing by issuing loans. It is a system in which banks lend to one another to create a growing debt pyramid that inflates the financial assets they have available to buy and sell countries and companies and finance mega-mergers and acquisitions.

Rampant political corruption, most of it legal, has put the public interest on the auction block and turned politics in the United States into a meaningless charade. The more unequal the distribution of wealth the more dominant the voice of big money interests in the political process and the more the rules are skewed to further favor the wealthy. It was evident in the 2000 presidential election that it made little difference to Big Money which of the two major party candidates won. They owned them both.

A poll commissioned by The Nation magazine and the Institute for Policy Studies found that a number of issues of deep concern to the majority of Americans were mentioned only rarely or not at all by either of the two major party candidates. These included how to reduce the gap between rich and poor (91 percent) and provide health insurance to the poor (74 percent).

Pursue a public interest cause relating to food or auto safety, fuel efficiency, genetic engineering, environmental protection, internet privacy, gun control, health care reform, teen smoking, water purity, the minimum wage, violence on television, recycling – you name the issue – if your proposal might cut into corporate profits there will be a corporate coalition putting millions of dollars behind a campaign to sink it. They will hire "experts" to support their position, place op-eds and "news" stories that seek to discredit you, cut off your public funding, question your science, raise concerns about the cost of corrective action, and dismiss you as greedy and pursuing a narrow special interest.

Buying special subsidies and regulatory exemptions politician-by-politician and country-by-country is an expensive and time-consuming endeavor. Corporations have learned that it is much more efficient to use international agreements to circumvent national and local governments altogether. To this end the WTO was established with an announced mandate to establish and enforce the trade rules essential to prevent trade wars and protect the interests of poor nations.

As demonstrated by its practice, the real function of the WTO is to block new regulatory initiatives by national and local governments that conflict with the interest of global corporations and financiers and to roll back existing rules regulating trade, corporations, and finance.

Proposals up for consideration at the aborted Seattle WTO meeting in 1999 would have placed further restrictions on governmental action to:

- **Favor local over foreign investors**

- **Preserve national food security**

- **Protect forest and water resources from expropriation by foreign corporations**

- **Regulate speculative movements of international money**

- **Clear the way for privatization of public services**

America's corporate globalists intensified their lobbying efforts to re-establish their hold on the political process and quickly won a string of victories over the opposition of labor, environment, and other public interest groups. In May 2000 the US Senate approved the African/Caribbean trade bill. Then came the passage of a bill establishing permanent trading relations with China, followed in July 2000 by passage of a Vietnam trade bill. All were touted as measures to assist poor countries, normalize trade relations, and open foreign markets to US exports. The Wall Street Journal noted that the real reason the corporate establishment backed the China trade bill was to provide guarantees that would allow US companies to move more production to China with assured access to US markets. That, of course, is also what the Africa/Caribbean and Vietnam bills were about.

Next time you hear a corporation touting its commitment to social and environmental causes, find out how much it is spending through industry associations, campaign contributions, professional lobbyists, and public relations firms to:

- **Roll back social and environmental regulations**

- **Win new trade agreements**

- **Extract subsidies from government**

- Defeat citizen-led public interest campaigns, and

- Paint a green happy face on its misdeeds

Aside from the highly publicized anti-trust case brought against Microsoft, the growing political influence of the largest corporations seems to have all but eliminated concern within the US political establishment about the concentration of economic power. In the grand tradition of Orwellian double-speak, we are told that giant mergers will increase efficiency, enhance competition, and benefit consumers. As it turns out, the only certain winners are the deal makers. In many instances both shareholders and consumers end up the losers.

As Herman Daly, the founder of ecological economics, observed, we are running the global economy as if we were holding a going-out-of-business sale and America bears a special responsibility. America's prosperity is an illusion that comes at great cost both to Americans and to the world. It is a prosperity grounded in a cultural trance that alienates us from our spiritual nature and tricks our minds into using money rather than life as the measure of wealth and progress. America's effort to export this self-destructive economic model to the world represents one of history's great crimes against humanity and the earth.

Yet there are also new reasons for hope, signs of a stirring in the human soul, that the great sleep is giving way to a great awakening to life and its possibilities. Its most visible expression is in the streets, but it is also finding expression in a new politics, a spiritual revival, a rethinking and transformation of our social and economic relationships with one another and the earth, and the emerging leadership of a new generation of youth.

Source: *Making Money, Growing Poorer*
by David Korten

Economic World Activity

The 200 biggest corporations in the world control 28% of world economic activity,

but employ less than 0.25% of the global workforce.

Disney's chief executive Michael Eisner was paid $575.6 million in 1998, $25,070 is Disney's average pay rate.

The wealth of the world's 84 richest people is bigger than the GDP of China with 1.3 billion people.

"Companies must show more developed emotion than fear and greed"

Anita Roddick

it's all just numbers

Anita: "Give me a one-handed economist," said Harry S. Truman, complaining that all his official number-crunchers would say was "on the one hand... on the other hand..." Yet one of the problems with the prevailing official world view is that the economists have barely any hands at all. There is one way, and one way only, and no economic truths, no poverty statistics, no popular revolt can get in the way of those official blinkers. But as Economics Editor of *The Guardian* in London, Larry Elliott has flown the flag for a different way, reminding our leaders of uncomfortable facts and knitting it all together into a coherent series of alternatives. By failing to succumb to the No Alternative view, he has bravely done the world a service.

Larry Elliot Let me tell you a story about life, death, and profit. It involves some of the poorest countries in the world and some of the richest companies. It goes to the heart of how the modern world is to be run and whether the institutions set up to police the global economy are up to the job.

Eleven million people in poor countries will die from infectious diseases this year. Put a different way, it means that by the time you finish reading this article 100 people will have died. Half of them will be children aged under five. Just over a quarter – 2.6 million – will die from HIV/Aids.

It is easy to work out why the death toll is so high. Poverty breeds ill-health and encourages the spread of infection, and the world is awash with poor countries. Just as a starving man knows there is food at the Ritz, governments in Africa, Asia, and Latin America know there are medicines to treat these illnesses if only they could afford them.

But the bigger developing countries have found a way round this problem by making cheap copies of western drugs. India, for example, makes 70 percent of its own drugs, while Egypt, Thailand, Argentina, and Brazil have also taken steps to become more self-reliant in pharmaceuticals. Poorer developing countries also benefit because they can import cheap generic drugs even if they cannot manufacture them.

This should mean our story has a happy ending. It means more people get treated because the health budgets of poor countries go further. It means that developing countries have a chance to move into industries that have a higher technological component. And it means increased competition, putting downward pressure on prices. This final point – that the freer markets are the better – is usually the clincher when it comes to the economics of globalization. But not this time.

Enter the two other characters in our story – the world's largest pharmaceutical companies and the World Trade Organization. Four companies dominate the pharmaceutical industry – Merck, Pfizer, GlaxoSmithKline, and Eli Lilly, and they wield enormous financial clout.

The Big Four effectively operate to wield monopoly power. It is basic economics that monopolies lead to higher prices, which is why many governments use anti-trust legislation to break them up. To say that the Big Four do not like the idea of cheap drugs coming onto the market from developing countries is something of an understatement. More competition equals lower share price. But the financial muscle of the pharmaceutical companies also gives them enormous political leverage. So, during the Uruguay round of trade talks they lobbied hard for tougher rules protecting intellectual property, which provided patent protection for a minimum of 20 years for "new and inventive" products.

Where previously around 50 developing countries and several developed countries had excluded medicines from being patented, the Trade Related Intellectual Property Rights (TRIPS) deal made both pharmaceuticals and biotechnology part of the global regime. Infringements of the TRIPS agreement are heard by a WTO disputes panel, and unlike in a criminal trial, the burden of proof put on the defendant country.

In itself, TRIPS – a protectionist clause in what was supposed to be a free trade agreement – roused suspicions about the way in which the rules were being skewed to suit powerful interest groups in rich countries. However, some safeguards were included. Countries could cite a national emergency as a reason to infringe the TRIPS agreement.

Effectively, this provided two loopholes. Countries could either manufacture cheap drugs themselves using what are known as compulsory licenses to override patents, which is what Brazil is trying to do, or they could import a patented drug from wherever it was sold cheapest, the method favored by South Africa.

All quite simple, you might think. If the HIV/Aids pandemic does not constitute an emergency it is hard to know what would. The developing countries win, the drugs companies admit defeat, more people live happily ever after. If only. What is happening now is that the US is using every available means to close the WTO loopholes.

In part this has involved armies of lawyers crawling all over the 73 articles making up the TRIPS agreement, in part it has involved legal action. But it also involved 21st century gunboat diplomacy. For example, the US offers a special deal to the Dominican Republic for exports of textiles. It is now threatening to withdraw this privilege unless the country scraps plans for compulsory licensing and parallel importing. Brazil and India have been warned that they could face sanctions under America's bilateral Super 301 legislation.

The dirty work for the drugs' companies is being done by the US government, although there is little doubt who is really behind it all. But gunboat diplomacy is still a dangerous game, because there is a risk that public opinion will turn against Merck and Glaxo SmithKline in the way that they have turned against Phillip Morris and the other tobacco companies. Becoming an international pariah is not good for the share price.

The Big Four have a defense. They say patent protection is vital if companies are to plough vast sums into developing new cures for the diseases affecting poor people. In addition, they argue that the incomes of the world's poor are so low that they would not be able to afford even generic copies of patented drugs, and that the answer is some form of public-private partnership. Several of the big companies back global initiatives either by donating drugs or by subsidizing drugs provision.

But the arguments of the pharmaceutical industry do not really stack up. For a start, their profit margins were already fat even before the TRIPS deal came into force.

Secondly, research and development costs are dwarfed by money spent on marketing drugs.

Thirdly, only 10 percent of research and development goes on drugs that account for 90 percent of global disease, with the bulk spent on first-world afflictions such as obesity. Finally, the drugs made available at lower prices are limited in supply and are still more expensive than generic substitutes.

As Brazil has shown, it is possible for a relatively poor country to treat HIV/Aids if they can manufacture the necessary drugs themselves. The price of triple therapy treatment is $4,000 in Rio, compared to $15,000 in New York.

Almost 90,000 Brazilians who are HIV positive receive free treatment, four times as many as would receive the care if the country were paying full patent price.

The US has started proceedings at the WTO seeking to force Brazil to amend its patent law. Brazil, to its great credit, is standing up to the US bully boys in what is clearly a test case for multilateralism. One of the main charges against the WTO is that it puts profits before people. If the WTO backs the drugs companies, it will be case proved. What should happen is that the WTO should clarify its rules to give developing countries the right to produce or import medicines at affordable prices. If a country says that it is infringing a patent to cope with a national emergency, the burden of proof should be on the patent holder to prove that the country is wrong.

The WTO is not a law unto itself. Governments should write the rules, not multinational corporations. And if they fail to back Brazil, India, and Egypt they will have blood on their hands. It was once said that all that is needed for evil to triumph is for good men to do nothing. And what is happening here is evil. I have tried to think of another word for it. But there isn't one.

Larry Elliott is economics editor of *The Guardian*.

Spot the Difference:

CAPITALISM...

Long-term, systematic, and irreversible destruction of global life has emerged during the current advanced stage of capitalism. In other words, there is an uncontrolled and unregulated reproduction and multiplication of an agent in the host body that...

...AND CANCER

- Is not committed to any function of the host body
- Increasingly appropriates nutrients from the host body for its growth and reproduction
- Is not effectively recognized by the immune system
- Possesses the ability to transfer or metastasize its assaultive growth to sites across the host body
- Progressively infiltrates and invades the host body until it obstructs, damages, or destroys the organs of its life-system
- Eventually destroys the host

It's **clearly** a budget.
It's **got a lot of**
numbers in it.

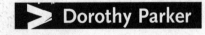 George Bush

If you want to **see** what
God thinks of money,
just **look** at all the
people He **gave it to**.

> Dorothy Parker

Anita: A society that accepts such a degree of extremes is asking to be torn apart.

Jeff Gates The wealth of the Forbes 400 richest Americans grew by an average $940 million each from 1997 to 1999, while over a recent 12-year period the net worth of the bottom 40 percent of householders fell 80 percent.

For the rich, that's an average increase of $1,287,671 per day. If that were wages earned over a 40-hour week, it would be $225,963 an hour or 43,867 times the US minimum wage.

Jeff Gates

THE WEALTH OF THE TOP 1% OF HOUSEHOLDS

1%

95%

NOW EXCEEDS THE COMBINED WEALTH OF THE BOTTOM 95% Jeff Gates

Anita: In the race to the bottom, these ten corporations are among the worst offenders.

Bad Business —
The Ten Worst Corporations of 2000

To get information on the 10 worst companies in America, which is censored in the UK, visit the *Multinational Monitor* website at http://www.essential.org/monitor/. Or better still subscribe to the *Multinational Monitor* magazine.

Always Coca-Congress!

Coca-Cola, the company criticized for selling un-nutritious sugary drinks to kids and for its employment practices, has bought its way into the Library of Congress. Russell Mokhiber and Robert Weissman challenged the move – and were barred from the Library for their pains.

On November 29, 2000, Coca-Cola made an "historic contribution" to the Library of Congress. The keys of the main hall were turned over to Coke, who decked the place out with its logo, stitched in red beside the logo of the Library of Congress.

Gary Ruskin, of Commercial Alert, was outside protesting. "It is not the proper role of the taxpayer-financed Library of Congress to help promote junk food like Coca-Cola to a nation that is suffering skyrocketing levels of obesity." He added that Billington had turned the Library "into a huckster's backdrop." Billington introduced Doug Daft, the president of Coca-Cola. In a loud voice we asked Daft: "Why are you using a public institution to promote a junk-food product?"

The next thing we know, we are on the ground. The Library of Congress police had tackled us. We were dragged downstairs, past the ambassador from Burma, and hauled outside.
"This is a private event," a man from Coke told the police. "I'm from Coca-Cola."

The police said we were to leave the grounds. And we weren't to come back. Ever.

Anita: It's strange, isn't it, that we can imagine solutions to global poverty – just as we can imagine the greatest buildings of civilization – but find that we can't "afford" them. Our imagination gives out when it comes to the simple matter of money. It endlessly seems to be the end of arguments: ah yes, what a pity, if only we could make it pay ... Luckily there are some people around who are busily trying to re-imagine money in practical ways, convinced – as John Maynard Keynes put it – "that what we could create we could afford." One of the most imaginative is David Boyle. He may be a journalist rather than an economist, but he has done more than most to get new, practical kinds of money taken seriously around the world.

David Boyle

The futurist Alvin Toffler asks executives what it would cost big business in hard cash if their new recruits had never been toilet-trained. They don't know, but it would be expensive.

"The minds of this generation are still so beclouded by bogus calculations that they distrust conclusions which should be obvious. We have to remain poor because it does not pay to be rich. We have to live in hovels, not because we cannot build palaces but because we cannot 'afford' them ... The same rule of self-destructive financial calculation governs every walk of life."
– John Maynard Keynes.

Keynes was speaking to the Irish government in 1933 at a crucial moment in Anglo-Irish relations, just as a trade war was breaking out across the Irish Sea. His speech became known as National Self-Sufficiency, and in it he outlined the idea of local finance. He urged that while culture should be international as far as possible, goods should be local as far as possible.

Here in a nutshell was the paradox of globalization – cultural hope but financial slavery – set out a good six decades before its time.

Keynes was also right about wealth. We use a counting system for the world that recognizes only some things as wealth – those that are easily translated into market terms – and simply ignores the rest. And as the global market increases, those other crucial aspects of "wealth" are ignored. Then they get forgotten.

Worse, the international money system recognizes only some needs – those that are most easily marketed. It ignores the needs of the poor, the young, the jobless, and the old. And ignores what they can offer too.

It just doesn't see it: the economic system is partially blind. It can see only what is rapidly becoming one international currency, that flows across the world's computer screens at the rate of $2 trillion a day – 95 percent of which is speculation.

It is froth, but froth with terrifying power over people's lives. As the world transforms itself into one global currency, the problem intensifies. The single money system ignores more. It flows to increasingly fewer people and fewer places, and, because it offers unsustainable short-term returns, it sucks up more and more of the world's capital into the speculative flow.

You can see the results even in a wealthy city like London, where everybody has to use the same global currency counting system.

That's fine for the international economy of course, the financial services sector. But there's another economy in London, which feeds off the pickings from the rich table above it, but is not necessarily part of it. It's the economy of the rest of us – those businesses and aspects of life so distant from the financial services industry as to be almost untouched by it.

The international economy brings in executives from all over the world, whose employers will pay their housing expenses no matter what, forcing up the value of London homes beyond anywhere else in the country, and pricing London services beyond the other economy altogether.

That's why London struggles to employ nurses or teachers or bus conductors, and because they can't afford to live there, so the basic services suffer. Worse,

London's rich economy threatens to drive out the poor economy completely. You can see the same thing happen in offshore financial centers where financial services have priced everything else into oblivion. In places like Jersey, in the Channel Islands, and other off-shore "tax-havens," it's the cuckoo in the nest.

Jersey's offshore status has made it rich in terms of money, and yet there is no longer a Jersey agriculture sector to speak of, and the tourist sector is well past its prime. Why? Because nobody but financial manipulators or banks can afford to live and work there.

But then there is a third economy in London too, and it is threatened because we don't see it. The third economy isn't really an economy at all: it makes up the crucial human transactions that build families and neighborhoods, without which nothing we do can be successful.

Economists are starting to call this "social capital" and market forces do not apply here. People don't after all bid for food at the dinner table. But without it, the police can't catch criminals, doctors can't heal, children can't be educated, and the other economies can't work. The futurist Alvin Toffler asks executives what it would cost big business in hard cash if their new recruits had never been toilet-trained. They don't know, but it would be expensive.

This social economy doesn't appear in the GDP, so politicians assume it's inexhaustible and ignore it. Yet it is the trust that underpins all the rest, but the international economy tends to drive it out by converting social transactions done by people for each other into cash transactions done by paid professionals.

That is the downside of global currencies the world over. What used to be done informally becomes part of the formal economy, whether it is collecting water or looking after your grandmother. That's why multinationals are forcing some of the poorest people in the world to pay for water they have collected free for generations. It is also among the reasons why the dumping of old people on the streets is increasing in Third World cities.

So is there any way of rescuing these hidden economies from the cuckoo in the nest? One answer is to give them their own currencies.

Every community in the world, however poor, however much it has been transformed into a vulnerable monoculture by the global currencies, has a wealth of talent and resources. It's just that the single international currency doesn't recognize them, can't market them, and discounts them – until even the people who live there think they're poor.

Increasingly the natural resources are being bought up by global companies, and these local resources are being slipped through people's fingers. But there are other untapped resources: wasted buildings, wasted equipment, wasted know-how, wasted imagination, wasted people – especially the young, the old, and the unemployed. Even local need is a resource, if there is the money to fulfill it. The key is to issue new kinds of money – most of it local, in regions, cities, and communities – that can bring those resources back in touch with the enormous weight of human need. Currencies are information systems: we need new information systems that start counting the world accurately – as no single information system can.

The models are already there. More than 15 percent of world trade is now carried out by electronic barter. There are more than 2,000 local currencies operating already, connecting people in the local economy even when conventional cash has disappeared like a tide. There are more than 500 time banks, using time as a kind of money that supports the social economy. There are the US models – like Ithaca Hours – where small towns print their own currencies.

We have the wealth. The brands may be owned by global multinationals, but the basic wealth – our ability to look after each other, our basic know-how, and our local resources – is still in our hands. Just.

New local currencies won't transform globalization into a wholly benign force overnight. But they can provide us with some independence, no matter what economic storms shake the world financial system.

David Boyle is a journalist and an associate of the New Economics Foundation. He is also the author of _Funny Money: In Search of Alternative Cash._

From **$1.5** to **$2 trillion dollars** now change hands **daily** in the **world's foreign exchange markets.**

Only some **2 percent** is **related** to **trade** in real **goods** and **services.**

Anita: The degree of control exerted by the world's governing economic bodies is the stuff of a conspiracy theorist's dreams – or nightmares.

Juliette Beck What do the Asian financial crisis, one billion people on the brink of starvation, $2.5 trillion in international debt, the decline of every major ecosystem on the planet, and sweatshops have in common? They are all outcomes of a global economy designed by the IMF, World Bank, and the WTO which caters to the interests of transnational corporations above and beyond the interests of all other aspects of life.

The IMF, World Bank, and WTO work together in an iron triangle to carry out the corporate agenda of privatization, deregulation, and "free" trade. Although the World Bank and IMF were originally founded to be part of the United Nations, they have always been controlled by bankers and economists from the United States and Europe. Under the guise of promoting economic growth, financial stability and development, the World Bank and IMF have forced more than 60 countries to open up their forests, minerals, fisheries, agricultural land, workforce, and financial markets to foreign investors without regard to domestic priorities such as food security; universal education and healthcare; the needs of local communities and domestic businesses; protections for workers, women, and marginalized peoples; and the limits on nature's capacity to be exploited and polluted.

A viscous and counterproductive dependency on foreign investment and the servicing of usurious foreign debt compels countries in the South to adopt policies that are harmful to their people. Countries are being forced to retool their economies to produce exports in order to generate the hard currency required to pay off loans from irresponsible lenders such as the World Bank and IMF. Instead of growing food for local consumption for example, countries now export luxury crops such as snow peas during times of famine and food shortages. Protection for indigenous peoples, workers, and the environment is sacrificed to attract the foreign investment needed to create an export-oriented economy.

The result of two decades of World Bank and IMF tutelage: transnational corporations have expanded dramatically – 51 of the 100 largest economies in the world are corporations – while global poverty, environmental destruction, and inequality both between countries and within countries have worsened. The World Trade Organization, founded in 1995 as a successor to the General Agreement on Tariffs and Trade (GATT), reinforces the opening of economies to further penetration by foreign investors. Countries in the South have been forced to accept rules they had very little say in designing. Even in the United States, only representatives of corporations are privy to the WTO's trade and investment negotiations. The WTO, while never claiming to be a "development institution" has promised significant gains from trade for its member countries. Yet the reality for countries in the South, in particular, has been very different. In the words of Victoria Tauli-Corpuz, director of the Indigenous Peoples' International Center for Policy Research in the Philippines, "The whole philosophy underpinning the WTO agreements and all regional agreements like NAFTA, MERCUSOR, etc. contradicts indigenous people's worldviews, concepts, and practices directly related to environment, trade, and development, and the way we regard and use knowledge and our core values and spirituality. The principles and policies they promote are antithetical to our core-values and beliefs... The World Bank and IMF have laid the groundwork for liberalization and deregulation, and the WTO is completing the task of removing all barriers to investment."

A reinvigorated movement for global social justice is emerging to challenge corporate globalization and break apart this iron triangle so that people from all walks of life, not neo-liberal economists in secretive institutions, decide the nature and aim of the global economy. The goals of this movement are to replace the inhumane and environmentally insane corporate economic complex with a system that values diversity, local autonomy, equality, a healthy environment, and democracy – not just the profit motive. Alternatives are sprouting from the recognition that human rights, environmental sustainability, peace, and equality are interconnected. One example of this is the fair trade movement. People can now purchase fair-trade certified coffee grown by farmers in the South who receive a living wage for their harvest and have access to credit. Fair trade coffee growing communities are gradually lifting themselves out of dire poverty and are living with dignity and hope. Just as past revolutions have fought for political democracy, this movement intends to democratize economic decision making at all levels so that people who have not benefited from corporate driven economic policies have a voice in redesigning them. The question is not whether to have a closed or open economy, but rather whose values are being enshrined in the global rulemaking? Is the goal to maximize the profits for the few, or to meet all basic human needs and protect the Earth? Global economic justice is not just ethical; it is key to reversing the demise of our ecosystems, our spirituality, our connection with nature, our health, our children's future, andhumanity itself.

Juliette Beck is economic rights coordinator at Global Exchange.

Anita: "When the capital development of a country becomes a by-product of the activities of a casino, the job is likely to be ill-done," said the great economist John Maynard Keynes. Goodness knows what he would say 70 years later, when all our lives are eked out courtesy of the rampaging casino of the international markets. I am occasionally accused of hypocrisy in the financial press because of how The Body Shop benefits from the international freedom to trade. Yet the truth is that the package of international regulations and mores known as "free trade" today is a caricature of free trade as it was understood for the past century and a half. Then it meant the right of free, equal communities to do business with each other, not the right of the rich and powerful to ride roughshod over the poor. That's the distinction made here by David Morris, whose influential Institute for Local Self-Reliance has done so much to redress the balance of power back to local people.

David Morris It wasn't tariffs that brought 50,000 protestors to Seattle's streets in November 1999. It was concern over issues like living standards, social justice, environmental protection, and political freedom. Free trade, as administered by the WTO, is no longer about how much tax to slap on an import.

"Perfection of means and confusion of ends seems to characterize our age." That insight of Albert Einstein's half a century ago aptly describes the current debate, or more precisely, non-debate, about free trade.

Free trade — a means — is now viewed as an end. Indeed, it has taken on the trappings of a fully-fledged religion: it is less an economic strategy than a moral dogma.

This explains why most commentators disparaged the 50,000 protestors who effectively shut down the WTO talks in Seattle. Most pundits saw the protestors as anti-trade. But the current debate about free trade is less about trade than about the nature of sovereignty, the role of community, and the reach of citizenship – a very different discussion from pre-1980s trade talks.

From 1848 – the year Britain adopted a free trade policy – to 1980, free traders conceded the right of countries to manage their own affairs. That included defending small businesses and family farms, enacting environmental standards, banning foreign ownership of key resources, and requiring outside investors to meet the needs of their host communities. The free trade debate was about tariffs and was largely unconnected to domestic debates about minimum wages, maximum hours, environmental and health protection, and social justice.

After 1980, the term "free trade" began to acquire a much more expansive meaning and the boundaries between domestic and foreign blurred. Free traders talked of doing away with "non-tariff trade barriers" – any regulation or tax that inhibited the movement of goods and services across borders. The rules have changed.

In an earlier time, countries were allowed to impose the same standards on importers as they did on domestic producers. That is no longer true.

In 1980, to their horror, Europeans discovered that two- and three-year-old children were reaching puberty. They traced the problem to growth hormones used to promote weight gain in cattle. Consumers in West Germany, Italy, the Netherlands, and Belgium persuaded their governments to ban hormone additives. In 1988, the EU imposed a Europe-wide ban on local producers. In 1989 the ban was extended to importers.

In 1998, the WTO ruled that Europe had no right to impose such rules on imported beef. Under the new trade rules, countries were no longer allowed to implement health and safety standards that "err" on the side of caution, even in response to citizen demand.

The WTO specifically prohibits any government from discriminating against a product on the basis of how it is made. A shirt is a shirt is a shirt, whether it is made from genetically engineered cotton or by prison labor.

Some 20 years ago, appalled by the brutal apartheid system in South Africa, citizens pressured half a dozen states and more than two dozen cities to adopt purchasing and investment policies that prohibited them from doing business with corporations that did business in South Africa. After he was freed, Nelson Mandela acknowledged the value of these efforts in accelerating the demise of apartheid.

In 1996, Massachusetts adopted a similar bill to one it adopted a decade before regarding South Africa, but this time aimed at the military regime in Burma. A dozen cities followed suit. But a federal court has ruled that because of the WTO, Massachusetts no longer has the right to enact such policies.

Earlier free trade agreements focused on manufacturing. Today they are slowly extending into all parts of societies. Indeed, the debate in Seattle was largely about whether and how to extend GATT into services like education and health and finance.

Originally GATT operated without an enforcement structure. The WTO, on the other hand, according to trade lawyer Lori Wallach of Public Citizen's Global Trade Watch, "has the strongest enforcement procedures of any international agreement now in force." World traders now have a cop on the beat.

We need to reconsider the value of the new free trade rules. Economist Paul Krugman says it is "a hypothesis, not a truism" that a country's economic fortunes are largely determined by its success on world markets. "And as a practical empirical matter," he declares, "the hypothesis is flat wrong." National living standards are overwhelmingly determined by domestic factors.

Paul Bairoch, an eminent Swiss economist, is more emphatic. "It is difficult to find another case where the facts so contradict a dominant theory than the one concerning the negative impact of protectionism."

The evidence is weak. The promised benefits are trivial.

- A massive report issued by the World Bank and the OECD to encourage countries to create these new trade rules predicted that doing so would add about three-quarters of one percent to the estimated world GNP in 10 years: one-third of the normal annual growth percentage of a typical country.

- Three years after enactment of the NAFTA, Mexico's trade with the US went from a modest deficit to a $14 billion surplus. Yet Mexico's economy imploded, living standards plunged, unemployment soared, and a wave of drugs and violence swept the country.

- In the 10 years after Europe embraced its internal free trade treaty, unemployment doubled. Growth rates fell.

- In 1997, Asia plunged into a deep recession when foreign short term investment, which had flowed in when nations jettisoned their controls on capital, flowed out at the first signs of economic danger.

For many countries, economies grew fastest during the 1950s, 1960s, and 1970s, when they operated in what we would call a highly protectionist fashion. Since adopting the new free trade rules, countries in Latin America and Africa have experienced economic stagnation or decline. In many countries, exports are up but living standards are down.

The free trade debate is no longer just about money: it's about the benefits of local culture and community and the rights of citizens. Let's hope that the battle in Seattle finds its way into the political debate, so that the "religion" of free trade can be examined more closely.

David Morris is vice president of the Institute for Local Self-Reliance and director of the New Rules Program for ILSR.

This is different from any kind of government democratic societies are familiar with.

- It operates in secret. The judges that sit on the WTO panels are appointed. They meet behind closed doors. They hear no outside witnesses. Their proceedings are not made public.

- WTO judges are not chosen because of their expertise in the subject they are ruling on, but for their adherence to the tenets of free trade.

- Only governments (and in the case of NAFTA, corporations) can bring a case to the trade panels. Citizen organizations, individuals, and local governments cannot.

- This government can only overturn laws. It cannot enact them.

- The WTO allows nations to enact laws that are weaker than a global standard but not stronger.

- The new planetary constitution includes no Bill of Rights.

- The WTO offers no democratic process for change. It can be amended, but only from within.

Anita: If the fall-out from the globalizing of business is most likely to affect the future, then it makes perfect sense that it's the young who should be most aware and active. That's why an organization like People & Planet offers such hope. It's the largest student network in Britain, consisting of groups in over 70 percent of UK universities and colleges and over 150 sixth forms, alongside commitments from members of the public. When it was set up in 1969, its original aim was to raise money for overseas aid but it soon became obvious that it was just as critical to raise awareness if the goal of long term change was to be realized. Now People & Planet exists to educate and empower students to take effective action on the root causes of social and environmental injustice.

People and Planet

Trade is essential to help poor economies develop. But it must be managed so as to be sustainable, democratically accountable, and beneficial to the poor. So we need global, rules-based trade regulations to avoid a vicious free-for-all. One thing we don't need is the new GATS proposals now being negotiated, which could block government efforts to manage natural resources, promote local development, and protect vulnerable groups.

In 1994, most countries signed the General Agreement on Trade in Services. It created a framework for the promotion of free trade, defined very broadly to cover "not just cross-border trade but every possible means of supplying a service." Over 2001 and 2002, that framework is going to be fleshed out with a huge expansion of GATS negotiated at the World Trade Organization. The aim is worldwide liberalization of services with new limits on the powers of governments to regulate services, and new freedoms for corporations.

"Services" have been defined as anything you cannot drop on your foot. They include health care, education, water, energy, and tourism. It's by regulating "services" that governments control commercial activity in order to pursue environmental and social goals such as conserving natural resources or protecting vulnerable people. But the multinationals want access to the huge service markets currently controlled or owned by governments. Enormous profits could be made if these markets were opened via deregulation and privatization. The previously obscure GATS is the corporate means to guarantee this end. It has been defined by the European Commission as "first and foremost an instrument for the benefit of business."

GATS is being enthusiastically pushed by the "quad" group (the US, Japan, Canada, and the European Union). GATS advocates within these governments regard a diminishing of their power to regulate as a price worth paying so that their own multinationals benefit from service markets abroad. Developing countries are less enthusiastic. Many only signed in 1994 because they were assured they would not be forced to liberalize any sectors they didn't want to.

One of GATS' driving forces is the removal of trade barriers, broadly defined to include any "law, regulation, rule, procedure, decision, or administrative action... applied by a central, regional or local government" which could give domestic companies advantages over foreign ones. GATS negotiators are proposing that governments be forced to justify their regulations with a "necessity" test to prove they are "legitimate." So far, the GATS' idea of a legitimate criterion is "economic efficiency." "Safeguarding the public interest" didn't make the grade.

GATS rules are enforced via the WTO. One country can challenge another, and the offender can suffer trade sanctions and penalties. Inevitably, the challenger and the challenged are rarely equal. But inequality is a signature of the GATS debate. The new proposals will increase the pressure for public services such as health and education to be privatized, which means that the poor could be denied basic services.

One possible future was glimpsed in Bolivia's 1999 privatization of water in Cochabamba. The companies that took over tripled prices, and even collecting rainwater became illegal without a permit. For many, water cost more than food. Tens of thousands rioted and the State Governor resigned. Eventually, the privatization was reversed (which would be illegal under new GATS proposals).

Some governments claim that the GATS exemption for non-competitive and non-commercial services means public services are protected. However, most public services have private competitors (schools, hospitals etc) and so could fall within GATS. This is confirmed by the WTO itself, regarding hospitals. It is also implicit in the US's desire to access service areas such as health, energy, and education, which are mainly in the public sector.

With its secrecy, its arrogance, and its flagrant disregard for local communities, the GATS typifies the worst traits of global business. The choices we make about regulation of services define the kinds of societies we want to live in. The threat the GATS poses to our freedom to make such choices is also a threat to democracy.

People and Planet

A **Government** that robs **Peter** to pay **Paul** can **always** depend upon the **support** of **Paul.**

George Bernard Shaw

One possible future was glimpsed in **Bolivia's 1999** privatization of **water** in **Cochabamba**. The **companies** that **took over** tripled prices, and even collecting rainwater became **illegal** without a **permit**. For many, **water** cost **more** than **food**.

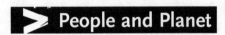 People and Planet

The Twelve Commandments

Anita: If big business continues to operate without a code of conduct, then God help us all.

1 Regulate transnational corporations and financial markets to curb speculation; money laundering; trade in arms and illegal drugs; corporate tax evasion; the international sale of chemicals and drugs banned in a corporation's home country; and anti-competitive practices such as price-fixing cartels.

2 Establish rules and institutions to give access to beneficial environmental, health, and other technologies – especially to low income people and countries.

3 Provide safeguards to prevent the international migration of invasive alien species; the pirating of indigenous knowledge; the patenting of life forms; the reckless introduction of genetically modified organisms into food supplies and the environment; and the use of child and slave labor to subsidize export production.

4 Establish ways individuals and communities harmed by the reckless actions of local subsidiaries of global corporations can sue to recover damages from the corporate parent.

5 Eliminate market-distorting export and international transport subsidies.

6 Establish a strong international anti-trust regime to coordinate national actions aimed at breaking up global concentrations of corporate power.

7 Strengthen local, national, and international food security through reforms that increase local and national food self-reliance; strengthen local ownership and protection of agricultural lands; encourage the use of sustainable organic methods; protect family farms; increase genetic diversity and prohibit the use of subsidized food exports by one country to undermine the food security of another.

8 Restore the democratic right of people to regulate financial and trade flows across their nation's borders, and to set the terms and standards by which others will be allowed to do business within their domestic economy.

9 Eliminate the debilitating international debts of low income countries and bring trade and international financial accounts into balance between countries.

10 Require global corporations to adhere to the highest international, local, or home country standards regarding human rights, labor, environment, health, and safety.

11 Provide a framework for sharing renewable resources fairly and phasing out reliance on non-renewable resources.

12 Penalize countries that attack others by dumping products at prices substantially below the real costs of production; use bullying tactics to force a country to open its markets to products it considers harmful or unnecessary; or disrupt a country's economy by unilaterally imposing an economic embargo not sanctioned by the UN General Assembly.

Institute for Local Self Reliance

www.ilsr.org

Grass roots — two words which resonate through this book, tellingly dictionary-defined as "the common people not ordinarily regarded as politically influential." Which just goes to show that the reality reflected by dictionaries is not necessarily close to contemporary truths. Fact is, it's at the grass roots level that the future is taking shape in many places around the world. And it's organizations like the Institute for Local Self Reliance that are helping it happen.

ILSR started out in Washington DC in the early 1970s as one single townhouse, which was remade as a working model in microcosm of a self-reliant community. At the time, it was a novel idea because sustainable self-sufficiency was the sort of idea you'd expect to find in the country rather than the city. As that idea was rolled out, first to the neighborhood, then to other cities and regions, ILSR became a national organization but its focus continued to be the grass roots — small communities, small businesses, farmers, and local communities. Its vision offered a prototype for the think global/act local recipe.

Since those early years, ILSR has created more blueprints for extracting the maximum value from local human, capital, and natural resources. Take energy, for example. ILSR's painstaking research established that 85 cents of every energy dollar "leaked" out of the community, which meant that energy conservation should play a key role in urban economic development strategies. The city of Baltimore was used as a template to investigate the potential for energy conservation and solar energy in a major city.

That is one illustration of ILSR's faith that our communities can be turned into much more productive places with the proper public policies. The key is waste management. ILSR defines waste not only as materials we throw away (eg garbage) but as available resources we do not harness (eg wind and sunlight).

Again, with its convincingly detailed reports, the organization was instrumental in engineering a switch from incinerators to recycling during the early 80s.

ILSR combines research and action. It turns its reports into economically viable strategies. The titles alone of those reports give a glimpse of the possibilities ILSR has explored: "Substituting Agricultural Materials for Petroleum-Based Industrial Products"; "Getting from Here to There: Building a Rational Transportation System"; "Free Trade: The Great Destroyer" or "The Carbohydrate Economy: Making Chemical and Industrial Materials from Plant Matter." With the concept of sustainable development a focus of conservationists in the new century, ILSR has been playing a key role in creating recipes for natural resource protection. It has been been actively involved in the debate about GATT and NAFTA. While it maintains that global rules to govern commerce are needed, these rules should be designed to encourage sustainable communities rather than merely to encourage greater mobility.

Deb Abbey & Michael C. Jantzi

Every dollar in your bank account, every pound in your pension plan, every yen in your insurance policy is invested. You may even have stocks yourself. All this money bounces around the world's stock exchanges, earning interest for you and its managers. But what does your money do while you are asleep? Who benefits from your investment? Is it spent on arms, tobacco, stripping the world's rainforests, or polluting its seas? Ethical investment is a way of ensuring that your money is spent the way you want it spent.

The oppressed and impoverished Maya-Chorti peoples of north-west Honduras are benefiting from a relationship between Oxfam and the ethical investment brokers, Friends Provident. For every new Friends Provident product that is sold as a result of its relationship with Oxfam it makes a donation of £80. With the money raised Oxfam has helped the Maya-Chorti to shoot a video to raise awareness of their needs. Oxfam are also helping Maya-Chorti communities to re-establish and improve agricultural production following the devastating effects of Hurricane Mitch.

www.friendsprovident.co.uk/oxfam

Ethical Investors Group has established itself as the UK's leading campaigner and advocate for Cruelty Free Money. When Ethical Investors Group was founded in 1989, there were no "cruelty free" investment funds available. Since then, its ongoing campaigning and discussions with investment and insurance companies has persuaded a number of the institutions to apply strict "cruelty free" criteria to their investments.

www.ethicalinvestors.co.uk

WWF joined forces with other NGOs, including Trillium Asset Management, to support a shareholder resolution at BP Amoco's Annual General Meeting. Resolution 12 called on the company to halt plans to drill for oil in the coastal plain of Alaska's Arctic National Wildlife Refuge and to switch resources to renewables – 13 percent of the shares voted supported the resolution. This rewarding result provides a strong foundation for further shareholder pressure. The BP AGM was the first time WWF-UK had used its shareholdings to put pressure on a company to improve its environmental performance.

This **country** can not afford to be **materially** rich and **spiritually poor**

 John F. Kennedy

Take it Personally

Don't give up. We can create our own currencies if we need to. We don't have to wait around for the banks or governments to do it for us.

Remember that everything you spend is a vote for the company you spend it with – wherever possible, keep it local.

Experiment with new kinds of money: can you extend your baby-sitting circle to other self-help services, for example?

Join your local time bank, and start earning "time CREDITS" by helping out in your local community. If you don't have a time bank, link up with a local school, library, community center, or health center and start one (more details: www.timedollar.org).

Get them to carry out a local skill survey, especially among the young, old, and isolated, and find out just what resources there are locally, and how they can be aligned with people's needs if they are measured with a new currency based on time.

- Persuade businesses to back their local communities by accepting time dollars for some services.

- Join your local currency or Local Exchange and Trading Scheme (LETS) if you have one. Find out at your local library.

- Persuade local business to take part too, bartering their spare resources and surplus stock.

- Find out more about new kinds of money (try, for example: www.transaction.net).

Books:

The 50 Best Ethical Stocks for Canadians

High Value Investing Macmillan Canada 2001 by Deb Abbey and Michael C. Jantzi. The 50 Best series for Canadians identifies the best stocks in the crowded world of investment opportunities. Whether it's blue chips, Internet stocks, small-caps or ethical stocks, the 50 Best series identifies the companies people should consider to build a profitable portfolio. Each book examines all of the stocks Canadians can invest in, both in Canada and around the world, and uses strict performance criteria to select only those that are worthy of the '50 best' designation.

Funny Money

In Search of Alternative Cash by David Boyle

Democracy at Risk

Rescuing Main Street from Wall Street by Jeff Gates

Natural Capitalism

The Next Industrial Revolution by Paul Hawken, Amory B Lovins, and L Hunter Lovins

Websites:

Calvert Group   www.calvertgroup.com

Known for offering the largest family of socially-screened mutual funds as well as award winning tax-free investment products, Calvert Group, Ltd. has quickly evolved from a single-fund management company in 1976 to become one of the Washington DC area's largest mutual fund management firms with approximately $6.7 billion in assets under management for over 200,000 investors.

NPI www.npi.co.uk/globalcare

As a long-term stakeholder in business, NPI is well placed to open a debate with companies about pressing environmental concerns. In recent years NPI has taken a progressive view on corporate governance issues.

FAIR www.fair.org

A national media watch group that has been offering well-documented criticism of media bias and censorship since 1996.

Ethical Investment Research Service www.eiris.org

The Ethical Investment Research Service (EIRIS) was set up in 1983 with the help of churches and charities which had investments and needed a research organization to help them put their principles into practice.

Social Investment Forum www.socialinvest.org

This site offers comprehensive information, contacts, and resources on socially-responsible investing

Ethical Investment Co-operative www.ethicalmoney.org

The Ethical Investment Co-operative is a firm of Independent Financial Advisers, dedicated solely to Socially Responsible Investment (SRI). It serves a range of clients, from individuals and charities, to trade unions and pressure groups. It believes in the issues underlying ethical investment – namely those of human rights, social justice, sustainability, and corporate accountability. It sees SRI as the ideal tool to bring about positive change in these areas.

Magazines:

Multinational Monitor www.essential.org

Monthly magazine that features exposes of global corporations.

Red Pepper www.redpepper.org.uk

Red Pepper is a magazine of information, campaigning, and culture. It provides a forum for the left to debate ideas and action. It encompasses a broad range of views.

An **error** does **not** become **truth** by **reason** of **multiplied** propogation, nor does the **truth** become **error** because **nobody** will **see it**

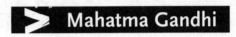 Mahatma Gandhi

A Buddhist Perspective

Anita: Spirituality and science have the same message for us: the essence of life on earth is interconnectedness. As Santikaro Bhikku says, "our real hope is in each other." Global business defies that. It divides rather than unites with its emphasis on short-term profit for the few over long-term gain for the many. But there is an antidote in the innate optimism of human beings. Our ideal is a holistic union of mind, body and spirit. The achievement of that union has become a quest for thousands of men and women all over the world. Infiltrating and redefining all areas of human endeavour, from fine art to quantum physics, it recognizes the rich seam of spirituality running through every aspect of daily life as an active, energizing principle.

Santikaro Bhikku The Four Noble Truths are the framework or overall map for the Buddha's Way. They encourage us to recognize and explore the simple fact that there is suffering in our lives, and question whether suffering is necessary or inevitable. They challenge us to explore the causes of suffering that exist within us as individuals and within our social institutions and structures. They offer a vision of hope that suffering ends when its causes are released. Finally, there is a way of life that brings to an end this suffering – that way is the Eight-fold Path.

Applied to globalization, these truths raise questions such as:

- In which ways is globalization a form of suffering today? Are there aspects of globalization that are truly happy, just, and peaceful? Or is it thoroughly decadent?

- How does globalization create more suffering? Does globalization ameliorate suffering in any way?

- What forms of globalization, if any, would be of greater benefit to life, for example, true global peace, harmony, and justice?

- **How do we live within the various forms of globalization so that we do not suffer more for it and how do we collectively practice "right globalization"?**

A central natural principle found within the Four Noble Truths is Dependent Co-origination. We observe the fact that all things are created, concocted, and influenced by other things. While this was a fairly radical perspective 2,600 years ago, it now seems commonplace due to the influence of modern science. Nevertheless, even today people overlook the pervasiveness of this fact, and further restrict it to material – often simplistic, linear, and mechanistic – causes.

Buddhism takes this conditioned impermanence as the central fact of life, as the Natural Law that governs all of nature. Nothing happens by itself; all things are dependent upon other things. Thus, we – all of nature – are woven together in rich, vast, complex systems of relationship. We are all inter-connected, all part of the same nature or Dharma.

Looking from this perspective, we might say that globalization occurred with the creation of the universe. Everything has been interconnected from the beginning. This perspective can help us to avoid some of the more polemical or divisive arguments about globalization, such as those who paint it in entirely putrid colors, overlooking the spread of democracy and human rights principles. Also, it situates the modern aspects of globalization within the larger cosmic process. This radically interconnected universe is much vaster than any mess we humans can create.

It is crucial to recognize that the current awareness of globalization concerns the unprecedented interweaving of economic and political relationships across the planet, and that these relationships have concentrated unprecedented power in the hands of a tiny corporate-bureaucratic-political elite.

It used to be safe to take the "ecological globalization" for granted. After all, it supplied all of our needs. Conversely, political and economic globalization has undermined the ability of global and local ecosystems to support us. It has also tattered the old webs of local commerce and community that gave our ancestors some control over their daily lives. This more recent globalization now offers itself to be taken for granted. Is it safe to do so?

Buddhist teachings broadly distinguish two kinds of strength or power: the power of wisdom, compassion, and selflessness; and the power of selfishness in the form of greed, hatred, and delusion. As we see great economic and political power accumulated in financial centers like Bangkok, Tokyo, London, and New York, we question whether it is selfless power or selfish power. It appears that the primary motivation in this fantastic concentration of power is greed. And it frequently expresses itself in the anger of military might, which is propagated by the willful delusions of mass entertainment and the media. At the same time, the picture is neither simple nor unilaterally evil. Such power can, and occasionally is, used for the benefit of humanity. Nonetheless, overall it seems that its accumulation and expression creates too much unnecessary suffering.

Can this power be transformed into a power for liberation? We are willing to work with the tools of global power – like the World Bank, United Nations, major corporations, and influential governments – when they are genuinely interested in shifting towards health and peace. While some Buddhists still hold to the old paternalistic models on which Asian states have sought their legitimization, progressive Buddhists put more hope and trust in local Sanghas – communities. Things can be kept honest by the checks and balances of spiritual practice and living together on a daily basis. It is through strong local groups and networks that we are able to bring spiritual values like tolerance, generosity, simplicity, inquiry, kindness, self-awareness, wisdom, and selflessness to bear on social issues.

Ultimately, globalization is just another phase in techno-economic development that, as usual, is dominated by and tends to favor the elites of the world. While the middle-class, and occasionally even the poor, may glean some benefits from it, our real hope is in each other, not in another mega-structure, such as the WTO, especially one so strongly influenced by greed, competition, and selfishness. Recognizing where real hope lies is the way forward for humanity. This will enable us to go beyond globalization.

Santikaro Bhikku

Eight-fold Path:

1. Right Understanding
2. Right Aspiration
3. Right Speech
4. Right Action
5. Right Livelihood
6. Right Effort
7. Right Mindfulness
8. Right Concentration

Magazines:

New Internationalist

"The people, the ideas, the action in the fight for world development." A long-established radical magazine, published in the UK.

www.oneworld.org/ni/

Adbusters

This magazine is published by Adbusters Media Foundation, which is concerned about the erosion of our physical and cultural environment by commercial forces. Through the magazine and its ad agency, Powershift, its mission is to transform our commercial media culture and direct it towards ecological and social awareness.

www.adbusters.org

YES! A Journal of Positive Futures

YES! A Journal of Positive Futures is published quarterly by the Positive Futures Network, an independent, non-profit organization fostering the evolution of a just, sustainable, and compassionate future. *YES!* encourages people to put their values into action.

www.yesmagazine.org

The Progressive (US politics)

www.progressive.org

Rabble (globalization)

www.rabble.ca

CovertAction (globalization)

www.covertaction.org

Websites:

Indymedia www.indymedia.org/

This is a collective of independent media organizations and hundreds of journalists offering grassroots, non-corporate coverage. Indymedia is a democratic media outlet for the creation of radical, accurate, and passionate tellings of truth.

Whole Earth www.wholeearthmag.com/

Whole Earth is committed to a vision of what's needed to challenge ingrained patterns and stale assumptions. Whole Earth shows you ways to take back your power and put it to use. You'll find information about restoring your local ecosystem, citizen advocacy, and socially responsible investing. Here are the tools for producing knowledge, and creating communities according to your own values and ideals.

Spoof world bank site www.whirledbank.org/

Corporate Watch www.corpwatch.org

Monitors transnational corporations and their social, ecological, and economic impacts.

Council of Canadians www.canadians.org

Member organization developed to advancing alternatives to corporate-style free trade and other issues facing Canada.

Institute for Policy Studies www.ips.dc.org

Independent center for progressive research and education; includes projects on global economy and peace and security.

Center for Media and Democracy www.prwatch.org

A non-profit, public interest organization dedicated to investigative reporting on the public relations industry. The Center serves citizens, journalists, and researchers seeking to recognize and combat manipulative and misleading PR practices. Publications include a quarterly newsletter, *PR Watch*, and two acclaimed books, *Toxic Sludge Is Good For You: Lies, Damn Lies and the Public Relations Industry* (1995) and *Mad Cow USA: Could the Nightmare Happen Here?*

The Foundation for Ethics and Meaning   www.meaning.org

The Foundation for Ethics and Meaning moves beyond outdated Left/liberal and Right/conservative paradigms, challenging the economic and cultural dominance of market-driven hyper-consumption; political, spiritual, and ethical apathy; and the ecological and human damage this worldview produces.

The International Movement for a Just World   www.jaring.my/just/

This is an international non-profit citizens' organization which seeks to create public awareness about injustices within the existing global system. It also attempts to develop a deeper understanding of the struggle for social justice and human rights at the global level, which it believes should be guided by universal spiritual and moral values rooted in the oneness of God.

Groups:

Public Citizen (WTO issues)   www.citizen.org

International Forum on Globalization (globalization)   www.ifg.org

People and Planet (globalization)   www.peopleandplanet.net

The Progressive (US politics)   www.progressive.org

Rabble (globalization)   www.rabble.ca

CovertAction (globalization)   www.covertaction.org

Documentaries:

Emperor of Hemp - Double J Films Production. It is based on the book *The Emperor Wears No Clothes* by Jake Herer and is about one man's fight for truth, justice... and a plant. What began as his singular battle has turned into a massive movement to educate America about this environmentally-friendly, beneficial plant. Can be purchased via Double J Films, PO Box 2178, Ventura, CA 93002, USA.

Books & Groups:

Corporations Are Gonna Get Your Mama; Globalization & The Downsizing of the American Dream by Kevin Danaher (globalization). Published by Common Courage Press. ISBN 1-56751-112-0

Captive State by George Monbiot. Published by Macmillan. ISBN 0333901649

Nation Without a State by George Monbiot. Published by Pan. ISBN 0330369431

International Forum On Globalization Tel: (415) 229 9350. Organizes educational conferences and distributes educational materials on Globalization.

The Ruckus Society Tel: (510) 595 3442. Trains activists in non-violent civil disobedience to help environmental and human rights organizations achieve their goals.

The Center for Third World Organizing Tel: (510) 533 7583. Trains community activists at their headquarters in Oakland, California.

The Midwest Academy Tel: (312) 645 6010. Runs 5-day seminars "Organizing for Social Change" based in Chicago.

The Student Environmental Action Coalition Tel: (919) 967 4600. Organizes college students on many global issues.

Agribusiness: the various businesses collectively that process and distribute farm products.

Biodiversity: the wide variety of animal and plant species in their natural environment.

Biosafety Protocol: an agreement signed in 2000 that gives governments the right to say no to GMOs.

Carbon Debt: the environmental debt rich countries have run up by burning more than their fair share of fossil fuels.

Davos: the Swiss mountain resort where the World Economic Forum was held in 1999.

Emissions trading: transferring the ownership of an emissions reduction to another party ie sources of air pollution can receive credits for reducing their emissions; these can then be sold, traded, or banked for future use.

Fair Trade: a means of trade whereby the grower/producer is guaranteed a just price for their produce over a guaranteed term.

G7: the seven leading industrial nations of Canada, France, Italy, Japan, US, UK, and Germany, whose heads of state and finance ministers met regularly to discuss and coordinate economic policy.

G8: the seven leading industrial nations outlined above plus Russia, which officially took part for the first time in 1998.

GATS: General Agreement in Trade in Services. A WTO agreement that aims to remove any restrictions and internal government regulations that are considered to be "barriers to trade" in the area of services ie schools, hospitals, rubbish collection etc.

GATT: General Agreement on Tariffs and Trade. An international treaty signed in 1947 to promote trade, notably by the reduction and elimination of tariffs and import quotas. It was superseded in 1995 by the WTO. GATT is now used as the WTO's general rule-book on trade.

Hotlinks: links on the Web between related words, phrases, or sites. The selection of one will open other relevant sites.

IMF: International Monetary Fund. The international financial organization set up in 1944 to promote international trade and smooth out temporary balance of payments problems between its members.

Kyoto: the 1997 climate convention in Kyoto, Japan, at which 37 industrialized nations (including the EU and US) agreed to significantly limit greenhouse gases.

Monoculture: the continuous growing of a single crop over a large area.

Montreal Protocol: the 1987 global agreement outlawing the use of CFCs.

Multinational: a large company that operates in several countries.

NAFTA: North American Free Trade Agreement. Signed in 1992, the aim of the agreement was to eliminate tariffs and trade barriers between the United States, Canada, and Mexico.

Neo-liberalism: a set of economic policies that favor deregulation, the rule of the market, privatisation, a reduced role for government, and elimination of the ideals of collective responsibility.

NGO: non-government organization. An organization independent of government control or funding.

OECD: Organization for Economic Cooperation and Development. An association of nations set up in 1961 to promote growth and trade.

Transgenic organisms: plant or animal organisms that contain genetic material artificially transferred from another species.

Transnational: companies/interests that extend beyond the boundaries of a single nation.

TRIMS: Trade Related Investment Measures agreement. This agreement limits the power of countries to dictate favorable investment measures such as stressing a minimum local content for raw materials.

TRIPS: Trade Related Aspects of International Property Rights. Part of a "free trade" agreement that provides patent protection for a minimum of 20 years for "new and inventive" products, including pharmaceuticals and biotechnology.

UNCTAD: United Nations Conference on Trade and Development. Established in 1964 as a permanent intergovernmental body, its main goal is to maximize trade and development opportunities for developing countries.

UNEP: United Nations Environment Programme. Established in 1975 to promote international cooperation in environmental issues.

World Bank: an international organization established in 1945 with the aim of assisting economic development – especially of the developing world – through the advance of loans.

WTO: World Trade Organization. Established in 1995 as a successor to GATT, the WTO's remit was to promote and regulate trade between its member states.

Page numbers in **bold** indicate an article by or interview with that person or organization. Page numbers in *italics* indicate a displayed quote by that person or organization.

Proceeds from this book are going towards supporting visionaries, grassroots groups and non-governmental organizations who are debunking the myths created by the World Trade Organization.

If you would like to re-use or reproduce any part of the text of this work then go ahead – email me for permission on book_duplicates@the-body-shop.com and I'll send you the copy. In return I ask that you use it well, credit the authors of any material you use, donate what you feel to be a fair sum to an appropriate NGO, and above all... **Take It Personally**

Element
An Imprint of HarperCollins*Publishers*
77–85 Fulham Palace Road,
Hammersmith, London W6 8JB

www.thorsonselement.com

First published by Thorsons, an imprint
of HarperCollins*Publishers* 2001
This edition published by Element 2003

10 9 8 7 6 5 4 3 2 1

Copyright © HarperCollins Publishers
Ltd. 2001

Anita Roddick asserts the
moral right to be identified
as the author of this work

Publishing Director: Belinda Budge

Editor: Gavin Lewis

Design: Wheelhouse Creative Ltd.
www.wheelhousecreative.co.uk

Picture Research: Carolyn Watts

A catalogue record for this book is
available from the British Library

ISBN 0 00 716173 5

Printed and bound in
Australia by Griffin Press

PICTURE CREDITS

Illustrations:
James Sparkes 1; Steve Chambers 169; Steve
Chambers/Henry Allen 63; Kary Fisher 33, 125; Emily
Phillips 138; Steve Villiers 171, 178.

Photography:
Nick Cobbing 41; Carlos Guarita 61 (center left); Mike
Goldwater 61 (center right); Ed Kashi 53, Shehzad
Noorani 61 (center); PhotoDisc Europe 52, 123,
129; Harmut Schwarzbach 61 (left); Gary Trotter 61 (right).

The Body Shop: taken from Full Voice, a pamphlet on
Community Trade, published by The Body Shop: Richard
Pullar 51, 81; Spencer Rowell 77; Tony Stone 82.